The Mythology of Sex

SARAH DENING

The Mythology of Sex

MACMILLAN • USA

A LABYRINTH BOOK

MACMILLAN
A Simon & Schuster Macmillan Company1633 Broadway,
New York, NY 10019

MACMILLAN is a registered trademark of Macmillan, Inc.

The Mythology of Sex was produced by Labyrinth Publishing (UK) Ltd.
Edited by Antony Atha
U.S. Edition Mary Ann Lynch
Picture research by Annette Balfour Lynn
Design and typesetting by Paul Griffin

Library of Congress Cataloging-in-Publication Data
Dening, Sarah.
      The mythology of sex: an illustrated exploration of sexual customs
      and practices from ancient times to the present/Sarah Dening
      p. cm.
  ISBN 0-02-861207-8
  1. Sex customs. 2. Sex—Mythology. 1. Title.
GN484.3.D45 1966
306.7— dc20

96–13515
CIP

10 9 8 7 6 5 4 3 2 1

Printed in the United States of America

PAGE 1*: Adam and Eve and the Serpent in the Garden of Eden.* Sicilian mosaic,
twelfth–thirteenth centuries.

FRONTISPIECE: *The Garden of Earthly Delights.* Hieronymus Bosch c. 1450–1516.

TITLE PAGE: The alchemical Queen, after coitus with the King, is impregnated with
the "child," symbolizing a stage in the quest for spiritual wholeness.
Engraving from Johann Daniel Mylius' *Anatomiae auri*, 1628.

CONTENTS

ABOVE: Anatolian fertility figure with exaggerated breasts,
hips and belly, possibly representing the Mother Goddess.
The flattened top of her head is a stylized depiction of a crown,
symbol of power.
Neolithic c.6th millenium BC.

CHAPTER 1

Introduction: Sex and the Myths of Creation

WHAT IS MYTHOLOGY and how does it relate to the sexuality of human men and women? *Collins English Dictionary* defines mythology as "a body of myths, especially one associated with a particular culture, or person." The word "myth" itself can mean a story, usually connected with divine or fabulous figures who behave in ways similar to human beings; but in a wider sense, "myth" describes a belief system which a particular group of people either accept as true or dismiss as superstition.

Each society shapes its beliefs about what constitutes proper sexual behavior and what is taboo to fit its particular social, psychological and political needs. All cultures have therefore evolved myths concerning reproduction and sexual behavior. For as long as these are current, they are accepted by the majority as absolute truth. Any other perspective is regarded as heretical, and people may be shocked by the radically different attitudes to sexuality found in other societies. In cultures where monogamy is accepted as the only basis for marriage, polygamy, which is just as much the norm in other cultures, is regarded as immoral. Unfortunately, human

OPPOSITE: *The Aphrodite of Rhodes*. Aphrodite, having risen from the sea, wrings out her hair. Hellenistic statue c.400 BC.

beings have a tendency to try to make everybody else conform to their own particular view, a trend which weaves its way throughout history.

One of the functions of a myth is to help one understand fundamental questions about how our own individual lives relate to the greater scheme of things. Whether we attribute a feeling of strong sexual desire to the influence of the goddess Aphrodite or to the state of our hormones, we are nevertheless trying to understand our experience in a way that makes sense. Ancient peoples personified as gods and goddesses the natural forces which make life work, and related to them accordingly. Realizing that you depend on the sun for life, you worship a sun god and observe rites to ensure that he returns each day from his nocturnal journey in the underworld. Then again, the earth is the source of the food without which you starve. You therefore worship the earth goddess and encourage her to be fertile, often through the performance of sexual rites. This is a wonderfully poetic way of approaching life, in stark contrast to our present-day mythology whereby the scientific method is often considered to be the only valid way of both asking questions and finding answers.

Carl Gustav Jung, 1875-1967, photographed in 1940. Jung, who had an unparalleled grasp of the psychological significance of mythology, considered the Christian Trinity incomplete because it excluded the feminine principle.

As human consciousness developed the ability to conceptualize, mythology grew more complex. More divinities came into being, whose stories tended to act as a role model for dealing with the major events of life such as puberty, marriage, childbirth and death. The images contained in these stories are what the great Swiss psychologist Carl Gustav Jung called archetypes. These are pre-existing patterns of behavior which we each inherit along with our genetic imprinting. The archetypes shape our attitudes and behavior and affect all aspects of life. They form the very ground of our psychic being, which Jung referred to as the collective unconscious, comprised of these universal human experiences shared by all cultures.

Gods and goddesses, heroes and heroines, characters who form the very stuff of mythology, are personifications of archetypal forces. The Divine Child, the Virginal Princess, the Wicked Witch, the Heroic Prince and the Wise Woman are but a few of the archetypes recognizable the world over.

The dramas played out by the archetypal players on the mythological stage were created in an attempt to resolve the kinds of questions human beings have always asked. From the earliest times, for instance, people everywhere have tried to understand the forces of nature – why the visible world is as it is and what the invisible forces are which make things change. All cultures have as a result produced creation myths, inherent in which are sexual elements.

At the beginning of history as we know it, around 20,000 BC, in the great river valleys of the Nile, the Tigris–Euphrates, the Indus, and the Ganges, lived settled tribes who grew their food and therefore depended on the bounty of the earth for their survival. Their attention was inevitably focused on the wonderful and mysterious ways of nature. They observed the sun setting and rising; the seasons rotating, bringing new life and crops each spring; the waxing and waning of the moon, which affected not only the great pull of the tides but the monthly cycles of women who bled each month. Perhaps the most mysterious thing of all was that a woman could gradually grow larger and then produce a baby. How was that to be explained? For that matter, where had people, plants and animals come from in the first place?

Having no idea of the relationship between sex and procreation, these ancient peoples assumed that women produced new life by themselves. They therefore deduced that the world itself must have been created by a divine woman, the Great Mother, who was the universe itself. From the start of the Paleolithic era around 20,000 BC until the Minoan civilization of the Bronze age of 3000 BC, this was the prevailing myth which informed people's understanding about life and sexuality.

Myth has always been enshrined in art, in storytelling and in dance. The myth of the Great Mother as creator is probably what inspired some of the

Map of Asia Minor, home of the original Great Mother Goddess.
Munster/Cosmographia, 1553.

earliest known art forms, statuettes made out of clay, soft stone and ivory which date back some twenty thousand years. Commonly referred to as the "Venus figurines," they represent ample female forms with large, often pendulous, breasts, big round buttocks and bellies, possibly representing pregnancy, and well-defined vulvas. Authorities disagree as to the exact purpose of these figures, although most believe that they represent the magical appearance of the pregnant female and are therefore fertility figures. The most famous is the *Venus of Willendorf*, c.20,000 BC, discovered in Austria, all breasts and stomach.

The magic of motherhood informed many myths and customs in these early times. Peoples such as the ancient Egyptians traced their descent through the female line and Pharaohs ruled by matrilineal succession. In the earliest dynasties, the name of the goddess was always incorporated into royal nomenclature, while scriptures of the time insist that great reverence is due to mothers. According to Babylonian law, anyone found guilty of a sin against their mother was punished by banishment from the community. In the period before the foundation of Rome, Italy was ruled by the Sabines who were matriarchal to the extent that even their kings did not know the identity of their fathers. In the pagan cultures of Britain and northern Europe, children took their mother's name. This was also true in the Orient. The imperial families of Japan were believed to be descended from the sun goddess and mother of the world, Omikami Amaterasu. In China, family names are formed from a sign which means "woman," a custom dating from ancient times when nobody knew who their father was.

The Great Mother in her various forms is credited with having taught mankind all the civilized arts, from agriculture to weaving, from writing to music and mathematics. In Hindu mythology, the goddess Savitri created units of measurement such as the day, the month, the inch and the second. Priestesses of the Great Goddess in both Egypt and Babylon were occupied

The Venus of Willendorf, Austria, c.20,000 BC. This is one of the earliest known representations of the mystery of female fertility.

Neptune heralds the birth of Diana, the Greek Moon Goddess and her twin brother Apollo, God of the Sun, representing the complementary feminine and masculine principles of life. From a French alchemical text, the so-called *Wordless Book* or *Mutus Liber*, 1677.

The Babylonian god
Marduk sets forth to attack
Tiamat, the Mother
Goddess, whose rule he is
about to transplant.

with writing and numerology. As far as we can tell, societies who worshipped the Great Mother were peaceable. Archaeological findings at Çatal Hüyük in Turkey which flourished during the seventh millennium BC offer an abundance of artifacts but no evidence of warfare.

Exactly when the male role in procreation began to be understood is uncertain, but most experts agree that it was some time after 10,000 BC. As people's thinking changed, so, inevitably, did the content of their myths. Mythology now began to give importance to representations of the archetypal masculine forces within the psyche. In using the words masculine and feminine here, I am aware that I am in dangerous territory. Since these terms are, by their nature, almost impossible to define, I shall keep to the simple approach of relating them to the imagery of womb and phallus. When used in this way, they are not value judgments but descriptions of different aspects of consciousness, of modes of being. Thus the feminine pertains to holding, containing, nurturing, drawing in, relating. The masculine encompasses whatever is goal-oriented, outer-directed, focused, confrontational.

In archaic times these qualities were polarized between the sexes. Early cave paintings depict men doing "masculine" things such as conquering and subduing animals, whereas at neolithic sites in Turkey dating back to the seventh and sixth centuries BC, statues have been found of a goddess supported by leopards as she gives birth. Goddess and animals are involved in the "feminine" condition of peacefully coexisting.

Today we know that each of us, whether biologically male or female, has both masculine and feminine qualities within his or her psyche, some apparent, some unconscious, and therefore dormant. There are assertive, aggressive men and introspective, gentle men, just as there are quiet, nurturing women and ambitious, dynamic women. Since antiquity these qualities have been projected onto gods and goddesses who may be protective and helpful or destructive and terrifying, regardless of gender.

Traditionally, the feminine has always been more associated with the feeling realm and the masculine with the world of the intellect. Women, however, do not have a monopoly on feeling. In my practice as a psychotherapist I have worked with men capable of deep feeling and with women whose intellectual capacities far outweigh their ability to relate. Nevertheless it is undoubtedly true that men, on the whole, have not sufficiently exercised their "feeling" function, that is the capacity to evaluate with the heart rather than the head. Had they done so, our civilization today would look very different. Instead, as we shall see, the realm of feeling has been largely devalued throughout history and left to women as their, inferior, domain. Men have tended to rely on the more objective faculties of reason and discrimination which, unless informed by feelings and emotions, can all too easily lead to disaster.

The change from a matriarchal society to a patriarchal society first appeared around around the fourth millennium BC in the cultures of Sumeria, Babylon, Egypt and Greece. There the creation myths gradually changed to accommodate the inclusion of the man's role in procreation. The emphasis still remained on the goddess but now she takes her son as both lover and consort. The myths of Inanna and Dumuzi in Sumeria, Cybele and Attis in Anatolia, Aphrodite and Adonis in Greece are primary examples of this development. Then around the same time came the great invasions of the Semites from the south and Indo-Europeans from the north. These were essentially nomadic hunting peoples, used to killing as a means of survival, and to conquering the areas they moved into. Since, for them, survival depended upon success at hunting and because the hunters were men, masculine needs and values were supremely important to them. In contrast to the importance accorded to the goddess in the agricultural societies they invaded, their myths were, inevitably, male-oriented. Their gods personified their own prevailing values, warriors like Zeus, the hurler of thunderbolts, and Jehovah, god of the Old Testament and the ancient Hebrews.

At this time of transition between the two cultures, the Great Mother (goddess) and the god of the male-dominated hunting peoples, the great goddess began to be both marginalized and demonized. Creation myths at this stage depict her as evil. In consequence, she is often killed by the god

Mosaic. From a Roman villa, Old Corinth, Greece, 2nd century BC. This has been interpreted both as the sun god Apollo and Dionysus, his fellow Olympian, who was the god of wine and ecstacy.

who then forms the world from her dead body. This is clearly illustrated in the Babylonian story of the young god Marduk who slays the original Mother Goddess, Tiamat. In earliest times Tiamat had been considered to be the universe itself. Now she appears in the form of a great dragon, an aspect of the devouring feminine, experienced by man as threatening. Marduk splits her apart and then refashions her into heaven and earth. The feminine is shaped by the superior will of the masculine.

Finally we arrive in patriarchal times dating from around 2500 BC. The god now creates the world by himself, either through copulation with himself, as in the case of the Egyptian Atun, or through the power of the Word as with Jehovah and narrated in the Book of Genesis. Some gods, such as the Brahman Prajapati, were held to give birth literally through the mouth, as a substitute for the vagina, while Zeus produced Athena from his head and Dionysus from his thigh. The early Hebrews also set out with grim determination to eradicate goddess-worship, a mission subsequently embraced by Christianity, and which continues to this day to affect us all.

In earlier times, above all the Goddess had represented the sacredness of natural life, and this included sexuality. Once the spirit alone came to be considered sacred, all that she stood for was necessarily devalued. The feminine now became identified with nature, the serpent, the temptations of the flesh. Sexuality had been transformed into something evil, to be feared and at all costs kept under control lest it lead a man astray and make him a sinner. Eve had disobeyed the word of God and women must henceforth atone for her transgression. Woman had, in short, become the enemy, an attitude which would from now on underpin Western attitudes to sexuality. The foundations of the myth of flesh as inferior to spirit were well and truly laid at this time. And there they remain to this day, a form of collective schizophrenia.

Yet the myth of the Goddess and all she stood for persisted. Impossible to eradicate, she was driven underground, where she survived, to reappear in Gnostic imagery in the early centuries of the Christian era as Sophia, the personification of wisdom; in the poetry of the mystics, where sexual imagery is used to describe union with the godhead; in the songs of the troubadours, as the object of courtly love; in medieval alchemy, as the *soror mystica*, the essential feminine element in the process of transformation. We owe more than we realize to those heretics through the ages who recognized the value and necessity of both masculine and feminine values. Many of them lost their lives as a result, sacrificial victims of a narrow-minded and ignorant patriarchy.

Such was the myth of masculine supremacy, best expressed in the narration of the creation of the world in the Book of Genesis, that for countless years it colored belief systems about procreation. Semen was considered to be the essential substance for procreation, the woman being merely a sort of incubator. The Greeks believed that the father planted a miniature human in the womb of the mother. Here it absorbed something known as "feminine matter" and developed until it was big enough to survive on its own. Aristotle, the Greek philosopher, 384-322 BC, proposed that the semen was a kind of essential soul substance, a potential human, which was planted in the mother's womb where it blended with her menstrual blood to produce the living child.

> *"The female always provides the material, the male that which fashions it, for this is the power we say they each possess, and this is what it is for them to be male and female…While the body is from the female, it is the soul that is from the male."*

Once their role in procreation was understood, men naturally wanted the same privileges as women. In early matriachal societies mothers had been deified and worshipped. As these societies evolved and changed, men claimed their due share of divinity. It therefore became important for a man to have many sons in order to create future generations who would in due course venerate him. The Chinese thought very seriously along these lines, believing that if a man failed to produce a son he thereby lost his chances of immortality. Inevitably, the patriarchal desire to found dynasties whose paternity was not in question meant that women, and women's sexuality in particular, had to be controlled.

Taking an overview across many cultures and throughout history, it becomes apparent that men have poured vast resources of potentially creative energy into attempting to control female sexuality. The consequent separation of sex from spiritual values has inflicted incalculable damage on women and men alike. In terms of our quality as human beings, patriarchy has not worked. Nor can we simply disregard the positive aspects of the masculine and return to a solely matriarchal position. Our work must therefore be that of exploring ways in which, mythologically speaking, God and Goddess can live in a state of mutual respect and harmony.

If creation myths begin at the beginning, myths concerning marriage carry the story onwards. Plato was of the view that human beings were originally without sex, each a whole unit. In looking for a partner to spend our lives with, we are really seeking the other half who will make us whole, as we originally were. A good deal of mythology reflects this way of thinking and uses marriage as a metaphor for union with our own eternal nature. The harmonious interrelationship of the masculine and feminine, in matters sexual at least, has always been better understood by the Eastern than by Western culture and is explored in detail in Chapter 4, *The Art of Love*. Their very different approach to sexuality did not involve the submission of the woman to the man. Rather it was based on the necessity for a mutual exchange of energy, each partner's role being of equal significance. This infinitely more intelligent attitude is reflected in the great Hindu myths and stories where god and goddess are presented as inseparable, forever united in a state of eternal orgasmic bliss. The Chinese equivalent is more abstract, embodied in the concept of yin and yang, equal but opposite forces. Although women in these societies undoubtedly did not enjoy the same freedom as men, feminine values were at least recognized and accorded some degree of respect.

In native societies, mythology is closely connected with the rites of passage marking the different stages of life. Ritual, which is the enactment of a myth, plays a central role, especially at puberty. Sexual maturity is recognized as the time to leave childhood behind and take up one's role as a full member of the community. This is not expected to happen automatically, as it is in our more "advanced" civilization. Rites involving isolation from the family, circumcision and perhaps bodily scarring, together with special instruction into the mysteries of being a man or woman all play their part. As a result, the young person cannot but be aware that he or she has entered a new stage of life. We who live by the modern myths of science and reason have often tended to dismiss such ceremonial customs as primitive, one of those curious things which tribal peoples do. Yet we offer no equivalent to the young people to help them grow into maturity. In the last chapter, I shall be considering ways in which we might address both this and other aspects of sexuality, in an effort to provide a new perspective on the sex war. I also suggest a new system of beliefs and values as a contribution to the myths of the twenty-first century. If civilization is to move onwards with more intelligence and compassion than hitherto, it is an area which needs our urgent attention.

CHAPTER 2

Tribal Societies and Rites of Passage

BECAUSE WRITING IS a relatively recent practice among many native peoples, information on their mythologies and beliefs about sexuality is not widely documented. Anthropologists and missionaries are our major source of knowledge, although the accounts of the latter are often presented with some degree of prejudice. To find proof of the limitations of our Western perspective, we need only look to other cultures and the diversity of their practices and beliefs, even today.

We must bear in mind when looking at the customs and belief systems of native people, that for the majority, the workings of human physiology were a mystery until recent times. Among many indigenous Australian people, for instance, the role of the father in procreation was unknown and not understood until relatively recently. One tribe considered that women conceived by eating human flesh. Menstruation was obviously connected with the ability to produce children since a woman, before and after the years of her monthly bleed, did not give birth. Menstrual blood was therefore seen as magical. Participants in religious ceremonies would paint themselves with red ochre which, in their eyes, then became the magic

OPPOSITE. Young girls taking part in an initiation ceremony, Ujiji, Lake Tanganyika, Africa. Henceforth they will be considered ready for marriage and motherhood.

A young Aborigine from Western Australia preparing for a celebratory dance after returning from a circumcision ceremony with the elders in the bush.

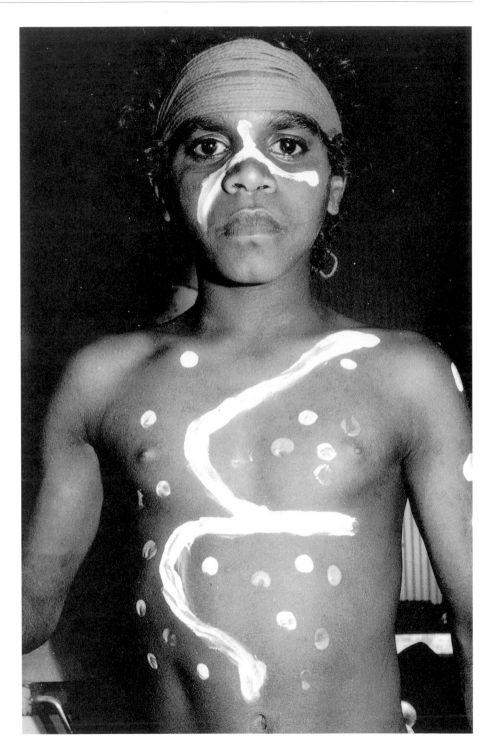

substance. In New Zealand, the Maoris believed that human souls were made of menstrual blood which, from time to time, remained in the womb and took on human form.

Because men also wanted to partake of this magic, most puberty rites for boys involved blood. Until recently in both Australia and New Guinea, boys underwent the rite of subincision whereby a slit was made in almost the entire length of the underside of the penis. The resulting blood was referred to as "men's menstruation." As long as the bleeding – their periods – continued, boys were subject to the same rules as women. This provides a clear example of the masculine envy of the female capacity to bear children that has been a feature of many societies since their very beginnings.

Throughout tribal societies, initiation ceremonies into the mysteries of life as an adult are the norm for boys and girls at the age of puberty. Circumcision is usually involved and was routinely practiced in ancient Egypt. Even today it remains a fact of life among Muslims and the

Mass initiation ceremony, South Africa. The rites mark the end of childhood. When they re-enter the community, these boys will be accorded adult status.

The third day of the puberty ceremony for a group of Dipo girls, Ghana.

Christians of Ethopia and is also a feature of Southern African initiations. The rite is the formal sign that a young man is now incorporated into tribal life and able to take on adult responsibilities, including marriage. Because the ability to endure pain is considered a test of fitness for manhood, the operation is performed without anesthetic. Without the requisite marks of initiation, a male would be thought of as a boy, unable to find a wife, since no family would consider discussing with him the serious business of a dowry.

In Australia, once a boy arrived at puberty, the men of the tribe, dressed to represent spirits, came to take him away from his mother for his initiation. It must have been a moment of profound psychological significance for the boy when he left the comforting embrace of his mother to face the ordeal which would mark him as a man. He was taken to the men's sacred ground where the age-old rites were performed, which might include circumcision, subincision or the drinking of men's blood. Episodes from the mythology of the tribe were enacted for him as a way of teaching him about his ancestral heritage. Finally, he was brought back to the village as a man, to meet the girl who had been chosen as his bride.

For girls, the period of initiation is often longer. It was a widespread practice, not just in Australia and Polynesia, but also in African tribal areas, for a young girl to be taken to a special initiation hut where she would be kept in seclusion for several months. During this time she would be instructed in sexual practices by an older woman and substances would be applied to her vagina in order to enlarge it. She would also be nourished with fattening foods so that, at the end of the requisite period, she might emerge plump, and she would also be ornamented to demonstrate her marriage value. Female circumcision was and remains a practice in many parts of Africa. This involves cutting off the clitoris and sometimes removing part of the labia minora, the aim being both to make the young girl "clean" or "a woman" and to ensure maximum sexual pleasure for the man she will marry. Although this custom deprives women of their own sexual pleasure and causes them unnecessary pain and suffering, a great many nevertheless accept it. Attempts to suppress this rite of passage, which obviously holds profound significance for such women, who are subjected to it, have met with strong resistance.

Throughout many cultures menstruation was surrounded by taboos. Because she was considered unclean or even dangerous, the adolescent girl often had to live alone at this time in a hut set aside specially for the purpose, and to take her meals on her own. In many parts of Africa, sexual intercourse was banned not only during the woman's period but at other special times. Hunters, for instance, when about to undertake a particularly important excursion, were not allowed sex with their wives. During her pregnancy, a woman was forbidden to have sexual relations with any man apart from her husband, who was required to be faithful to his wife during this time. During the last few weeks of pregnancy, the couple were obliged to abstain from sex altogether to prevent the husband from damaging the child's fontanelle. A nursing mother was advised not to conceive again, lest she drain her strength.

The Traditions of Africa

In terms of the myths which inform beliefs about sexuality, God is understood in many parts of Africa to be male, although there are also areas where a female deity is the primary God. In the Niger delta, a many-breasted mother goddess was worshipped, while for the Igbo it is the earth goddess Ala who reigns supreme. The Baga people of West Africa have a goddess called Nimba who presides over generation and new life. Because she is the source of fertility for both women and the earth, the continuation of human life depends on her blessings. Pregnant women are believed to be specially protected by her. Masks of Nimba play an essential role in agricultural rites.

Twins have special significance in several African countries. In Benin the divine role is occupied by a pair, Mawu and Lisa. Mawu represents the feminine principle, a goddess of fertility whose gentle, nurturing qualities relate her to the moon. Lisa is the masculine power, strong and warlike and

These head-dresses known as "Damba", representing a woman who had born children, were owned by Baga villages in West Africa. Until the 1950s they were worn by dancers in annual ceremonies to promote the fertility of women and the land. Now they have mere entertainment value. Coastal Guinea, early 20th century.

Dogon dancers of Mali.

more like the sun. As a result, there was a cult of revering twins in the area and a twin birth was seen as particularly fortuitous.

For the Yoruba people of Nigeria, great attention is also paid to twins. They are regarded as special, a source of good fortune to those who respect and honor them, but who are equally able to bring harm if neglected. The concept is a result of the Yoruba belief about what happens before birth. At this time, the child's ancestral soul kneels in front of the supreme being, Olorun, and tells him what kind of destiny it would like in the new life to come. Provided the request is reasonable, it is granted, and all the details of the person's future life are fixed. A multiple birth is therefore seen as the bestowal of a very exceptional destiny by Olorun. This holds true whether the twins are born alive or dead. After the birth, the twins' placenta is buried in a pot and the divination priest consulted as to the most appropriate sacrifices and rituals for the occasion. Should a twin die, a statue is made to represent it as a means of placating its spirit. Once the figure is ready, the mother brings it to the family, who gather with their friends for feasting and dancing. The statue is adorned with beads and shells for the occasion. From then on, it is treated in exactly the same way as the surviving twin, being washed, clothed and put to bed with it. As an adult, the survivor assumes responsibility for the statue.

According to the Yoruba, the god Esu is responsible for the well-being, or otherwise, of the sexual relationship between man and wife. Esu is a trickster god who loves to create havoc. Androgynous in nature, he is often represented by a closely linked pair of male and female figures. Like all tricksters he is capable of great mischief and can deeply affect a situation for better or worse, depending on his mood. Esu is thought to laugh when a man fails to achieve an erection. Yoruba believers pray to him often in the hope that he will leave them alone.

For the Dogon people, creation happened in a specifically sexual way. Amma, the creator god, made the earth out of clay so that it lay flat like a female body. An anthill represented the earth's vulva and a termite hill marked her clitoris. The story tells how Amma, being lonely, decided to have sexual intercourse with his new creation. However, as he approached her, the termite hill rose up, making it impossible for him to penetrate her. Amma's response was to cut it down. Then he proceeded to fulfill his desires. This myth is held to be one of the reasons for the custom of clitoridectomy for Dogon women, the other being the myth of the Nommo.

The Nommo are ancestral figures, the androgynous offspring of Amma. The original Nommo were the primordial couple, born as twins. Although each twin possessed both male and female characteristics, signifying their completeness, one had slightly more female qualities while the other was more male. Human from the waist up and serpent-like in the lower body, their bodies were green, the surface of the skin gleamed like water, and was covered with fine green hair as a symbol of vegetation and fertility. The main job of the Nommo was to counteract the havoc which had been wrought by the earlier trickster-god Yurugu. Born neither a twin nor an androgyne, he was therefore considered incomplete, a transgression against the divine order. In order to try and become whole he had intercourse with his mother, the earth, and as a result, chaos ensued. Desecrated by this act of incest, Mother earth lost the gifts of fertility and speech which Amma had given her and became dry and barren.

The Nommo came to her rescue by entering her womb and blessing her with the divine Word, which made her fertile again. For the Dogon, human speech has a similar creative effect. "Good" words leave the speaker, traveling on his breath, and enter the genitals of any woman who is

Masai Mara, Kenya. A traditional dance of the Kedong warriors. Until recently a Masai aspiring to warriorhood had to prove his worth by killing a lion with his spear.

listening, thus increasing her fertility. It is through the Nommo that the Dogon are able to come into contact with the supreme being. And just as the Nommo are andro-gynous, so, according to Dogon belief, is every child. From the moment of birth, children have both a male and a female soul. If they were to be left in this state, they would have no interest in pro-creation. At puberty, there-fore, the contrasexual element must be removed from the body, leaving a single soul. Ritual circumcision and clitoridectomy fulfill this purpose.

The Dogon have a very clear-cut attitude toward the difference between the sexes: men are men and women are women. Through circumcision a boy is thought to become completely male, free from the feminine qualities he had in childhood. Conversely, in the case of a girl, removal of the clitoris means, not only that she loses any trace of masculinity, but that she become ready for intercourse, in the same way as the earth in the creation myth. For the Dogon, a person who has not undergone these rites is not considered to be fully human.

The Bakongo people living in southwestern Zaire manage their morals with the aid of spirit helpers. A home is made for the spirit by fashioning a nail charm, the representation of a torso of a figure which has a nail hammered into it. The spirit now believed to inhabit the figure, known as a n'kondi, has protective powers and is able to detect adultery and other transgressions. A man might make a vow of loyalty to his wife by touching the lips of the image with iron. Then an iron or wooden peg is hammered into the image in order to activate its powers. If the man should subsequently break his oath, the spirit of the image will seek revenge and will hunt out or even kill the offender. The first n'kondi, called Funza, was created by the supreme god Nzambias as a kind of messenger.

Anybody who has been on safari in Kenya will probably have at least a

A Masai cattle herdsman
with his spear in the
Ambesoli National Park,
Kenya. His social status is
largely dependent upon the
number of cattle he owns.

photographic acquaintance with the people of the Masai and Samburu tribes. One of the unfortunate results of tourism is that the Masai rites, in particular, no longer hold the same importance as before. Commercialization here, as elsewhere, is beginning to eat at the soul of an ancient culture, one result being that their warriors are already no longer a disciplined fighting force. Let us hope that some of the more positive aspects of Western culture will benefit them, particularly in respect of the position of women.

A Masai women's myth tells how men and women were once equal. The women were warriors who were braver than their male counterparts, young men known as "moran." At this time, the women had no vaginas, just tiny holes through which they urinated. One day the moran needed help in waging war so the women accompanied them. As they sat around their separate fires that night, the moran crept up behind the women and pushed the sharp ends of the bows they carried into the women's bodies, creating vaginas. They then all copulated. The next day, the moran decided that these were just women after all and married them, at which point women lost their bravery and fertile life began.

There can be no clearer indication of the deeply inferior status of women in this culture than this story. In any tribal culture that depends on the hunt for food, warriors are all-important. Masai warriors must also deal with raiding and killing. In times of drought, it is their responsibility to move the cattle in search of water, a perilous process which may well involve encounters with bandits and lions. But the Masai take the elevation of the male to an extreme of chauvinism. Women have no status at all. They are seen simply as sexual providers and mothers, neither role being accorded any particular value.

Initiation rites among the Masai involve circumcision for both boys and girls. This takes place at about the age of fifteen for a boy and for a girl shortly after her breasts have begun to develop. A girl will shortly afterwards be married to an older man. Warriors tend not to marry girls of their own age. Many a girl, however, has had a warrior lover whom she finds far more attractive than her husband. Each warrior belongs to an age set, a group whose members watch out for one another, somewhat in the way Western men who have attended a certain school or university band together. Members of each warrior group are generally recruited at puberty for a period of about fourteen years and a young man is automatically initiated into the age set that is open at the time of his circumcision. He will remain a member of this set throughout his life, moving with the whole group through the various rituals.

The Samburu operate similar age sets, each of which is given a name reflecting the overall temperament of the group. Samburu boys are circumcised *en masse* at puberty and thereafter become warriors. Each warrior-to-be also undergoes rituals whereby he is separated from his mother so that his male sexuality may be recognized. From then on, he will no longer eat in his mother's hut. With those of his age set, he will go off at intervals into the thick bush to kill an animal with a spear, usually a buffalo or an elephant, and to spend a week or so subsisting on meat. Warriors are expected to be highly disciplined, and these "meat camps" are a most effective way of bonding the group.

Once he is a warrior, a young man is allowed to court a girl although he is not supposed to engage in sexual intercourse with her, to avoid a pregnancy – something which is considered highly shameful. Girls are given no choice in the matter of a husband. The Samburu have a custom reminiscent of some Polynesian tribes whereby, if a man can kidnap the girl during the time between her circumcision and her marriage, she then belongs to him. To prevent this happening, girls are usually circumcised the night before the marriage or even on the same morning. Unlike the boys, girls are allowed to cry during their ordeal, which is performed with a razor blade. Normally, her husband will expect to have intercourse on their wedding night, and no thought at all is given to the suffering she must inevitably undergo.

A man's obligations towards other members of his age set include providing hospitality to the extent of offering his wife as a bed-fellow. Any children of the union are considered as his own. Women are otherwise supposed to be faithful to their husbands and expected particularly to resist the charms of the warriors, who are often very beautiful, the "boy-toys" of the culture. Yet rules are made to be broken. If a wife is found to be unfaithful, her husband is not allowed to confront her or the warrior in question. He must put his case before the elders and abide by their decision.

Once the Christian missionaries arrived in Africa in the wake of David Livingstone in the middle of the nineteenth century, they started imposing their own set of myths and belief systems upon the indigenous culture, with some less than fortunate results. Christian views on nudity were totally at odds with what was considered normal by most Africans, who were used to going about either totally naked or only partially clothed, as befitted the climate. Missionaries encouraged girls in particular to wear voluminous garments to hide their breasts and bodies which must have looked quite ridiculous, as well as being rather unhealthy, in the environment in which they were worn.

Native American Indians

Because the North American Indian communities left no written records what we know about their culture, experiences, and attitudes to sexuality has been handed down through their very strong oral tradition. What is certain is that the many tribes, scattered over a huge area and faced with the necessity of adapting to considerable variations of both climate and environment, embraced an extremely wide range of behavior patterns and customs. As is usually the case in hunting societies, women generally occupied a low position, particularly as the female role in conception was not known for a very long time. It was thought that children were created through a spirit entering the woman and taking form.

In order to ensure the regulation of sexual activity, any marriage had to be made known to every member of the community. The parents and other relatives of a bride and groom played a significant part in the selection of a partner and in some communities it was the custom to betroth children and even, on occasion, infants. This was common practice among the Eskimos, although the harsh environmental conditions often prevented the children involved from living long enough to consummate the marriage.

Among the various tribes, the institution of marriage was based upon the system of totemism, which meant that a taboo was placed on marriages between members of the same clan. The nature of the actual wedding ceremony differed with locality and race. Among the Plains Indians where polygamy was common, the central feature was the presentation of gifts to the bride's father. In areas where the purchase system was not in operation, the wishes of the woman were consulted before her husband was chosen. Elsewhere, the husband had absolute power over his wife and separation and divorce were quite common. Unusually, marriages amongst the Huron were arranged by a council of mothers.

Sexual relationships prior to marriage were widespread in the majority of

Totem poles in Stanley Park, Vancouver, B.C., Canada. Symbols of the tribal consciousness of the Indian peoples of the Northwest Coast, they were carved and painted to represent family and group history.

Gods of the Dakota Sioux. This great tribe of the plains had a deep sense of the sacred within all the manifestations of natural life.

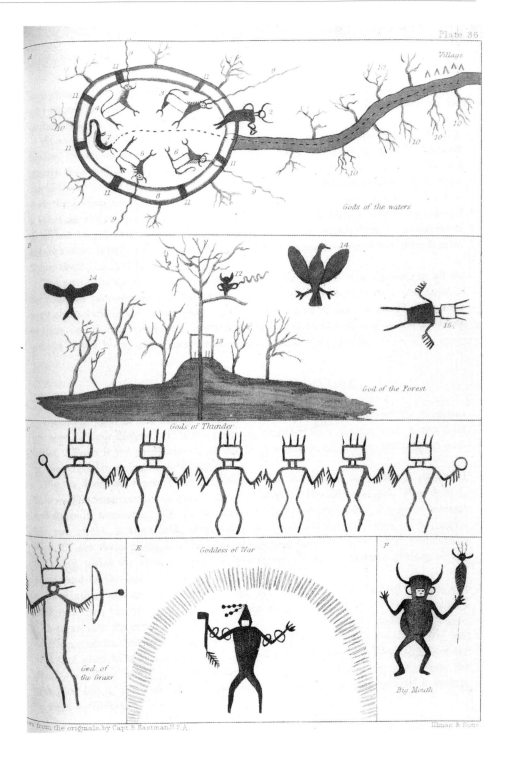

North American Indian societies, a notable exception being the Cheyenne. But this did not mean that young Indians were exceptionally active sexually. Girls were considered ready for marriage after their first menstruation while a man could expect to have a wife by the time he was twenty. Among the Plains tribes, however, higher-ranking families made great efforts to impose virginity on their unmarried daughters. In the case of the Crow, a specific ceremonial role could only be performed by a woman who had been a virgin at the time of her marriage and who had remained faithful to her husband since.

Among tribes on the Northwest coast, young women were sometimes confined to a boarded-off room in the house from the time of puberty until they married. The combination of virginity plus an unusually light skin would not only command a higher bride price for the girl but would also increase her chances of marrying into a higher-ranking family. Some tribes in British Columbia went even further and sent girls after their first menstruation out into the wilderness, where they spent a few years in total seclusion. The official reason for such a mysterious custom was that a girl of this age constituted a threat to anybody who saw her. On a more practical note, it would have served as a means of controlling sexual behavior and possibly birth in the community. Less extreme forms of birth control included the drinking of infusions of roots and leaves in the form of a tea practiced by the Navajo and the Hopis. As in many tribal societies, infanticide was also sometimes an accepted form of birth control. Tribes which needed to protect their food supply, and which suffered a high death rate among the hunters and warriors, could not afford another life to feed.

The Indian boy had his own initiation process, which took place at about the age of fifteen. Among the Plains Indians the boy would undertake his first vision quest at this time. This would usually mean being separated from the group and left in a womb-shaped hole in the ground, surrounded by sacred objects. He went without food or sleep while awaiting the appearance of the spirits who appeared in various forms. If he were fortunate enough to have a vision, it would help to define his identity as a man and his future role within the tribe. One Crow chief told how the Moon had appeared to him during his first vision quest and had instructed him to look upon it as his guide and protector whom he could henceforth always call upon for help.

The North American Indian bride had her price, and her social prestige

would be reflected in the amount paid for her. Her family would in turn bestow gifts upon the groom's family, often equalling the bridal price in value. The traditions surrounding marriage seem not so much a business transaction as a means of establishing social rank. During the nineteenth century, however, the acquisition of a bride became a much more obviously commercial enterprise because of the requirements of the fur trade. The women of the tribes in the northern Plains had the task of dressing the buffalo hides. Because this was slow work, calling for as many hands as possible, a man might purchase as many wives as he needed to keep up with the rate at which he hunted. A wife in this society was usually acquired in exchange for horses.

A man could also prove his worth as a husband by going to live with his future wife's parents and working for her father. After about a year, if he had demonstrated a satisfactory ability to hunt and earn a living in the manner required by the particular culture, he was then given the daughter as his bride. This at least had certain advantages from the prospective wife's point of view, however she might regard the partner chosen for her. In some areas a boy might be no more than ten years old when he went to live with his future father-in-law so his wife-to-be would have ample opportunity to get to know him.

Marriage by abduction of the bride, a feature of some Hollywood Westerns, was not very frequent. Women were sometimes captured during warfare and kept as wives, although they might alternatively be put to work as slaves. Some tribes in Mexico and Central America would enact a mock capture as part of the marriage ceremony. Eighteenth-century explorers reported that it was customary among many of the Canadian Indian tribes for a man to acquire a wife by exhibiting skill in wrestling. His abilities in this respect were considered more valuable than mere wealth. During the struggle between two rivals the girl in question would look on and perhaps enjoy a brief moment of satisfaction at being the center of attention. Women of the time otherwise held a very subservient position. It was considered quite normal for a man who was a good enough wrestler to take another's wife, the woman being given no choice except to submit.

Although the majority of the North American peoples practiced polygamy, the Iroquois were monogamous. Descent was traced through the female line and the women owned land and houses. A man, when he married, would move in with his wife. If he proved an unacceptable husband, she could divorce him by tossing his personal effects out of the door of the longhouse.

One of the better-known Eskimo customs was that of wife-lending, whereby a man would offer his wife for a night to a total stranger and sometimes to a friend or relative for longer periods. The beneficiary of this largesse would sleep with the wife in his host's bed. As the dwelling would have only one room, privacy was confined to what the darkness offered. Another widespread custom was that of two brothers sharing one wife. Often a younger brother would simply move in with an older married one. This form of polyandry may have been the most practical way of dealing with the fact that women were in the minority. The birth of a boy meant the addition of another hunter or warrior to the tribe whereas a girl was considered dispensable.

Incest was absolutely taboo in Indian North America, where the word for "sister" was also applied to all a man's female cousins. However, on the Northwest Coast, marriage between cousins was in fact preferred. If a woman had been left a widow it was quite usual for her to be married again to the brother of her deceased husband.

Among the tribes of the Southeast, attitudes towards sex were particularly liberal. Since it was taken for granted that both sexes would have premarital sexual experience, no shame or secrecy was attached to such activities. The only restrictions placed upon young people involved not violating the rules regarding incest or adultery. Within these same restrictions, a young unmarried woman was even allowed to charge for her favors. This was not considered to be professional prostitution; that was exclusively the realm of women who had committed adultery and been abandoned by their offended husbands. Although prostitutes were tolerated, they were very much looked down on. When an unmarried girl became pregnant, which happened quite often, the child was brought up either by the mother's family or the extended family. Should the girl prefer, she could have her baby put to death provided this happened within one month of its birth.

The inside of the lid of an Eskimo trinket box from Southwest Alaska. It is decorated with several sexually explicit scenes, along with animals, supernatural beings and hunting scenes. Despite the prevalence of sex as a subject of conversation, sexual symbolism was not particularly common in Eskimo art.

A myth of the Sioux Indians tells how a beautiful and seductive woman was courted by a young warrior. She accepted his advances and gave herself to him inside a cloud. When it lifted, the woman was alone. At her feet was all that remained of the warrior, a heap of bones which were being gnawed by snakes. Here is one of countless examples of the almost universal fear of feminine sexuality.

Among the Algonquins, men hunted while women sowed and harvested the fields, looked after the children and maintained the portable family wigwam. They could not understand the inequality of the roles Europeans assigned to the sexes. One Englishman reported the Indians' reaction to the white female's social function:

> *"They say Englishman much foole for spoiling good working creature, meaning women. And when they see any of our Englishwomen sewing with their needles or working coifes or such things, they will cry out 'Lazie squaes!'"*

The Navajo of the Southwest have a creation myth relating how the people emerged from a series of underworlds, finally reaching the Earth Surface. The myth has different versions, one being that First Man, First Woman and other Holy People held an all-night ceremony at the Place of Emergence, during which they created the world as we know it. From a "medicine bundle" they had carried with them from the underworlds, they put in place what they called the "inner forms" of all natural things, such as the earth, the sky, plants, animals and sacred mountains. Changing Woman was subsequently born into this new world and was impregnated by the sun. She gave birth to twin sons, created maize and then created the Earth-Surface People, the Navajo, out of cells she rubbed off her skin. In other versions, Changing Woman is the child of Father Sky and Mother Earth. Until very recently, the Navajo had a puberty rite for girls in the form of a chant celebrating the transformation of Changing Woman from a girl into a woman.

The Yanomamo of the Amazon Basin

For the Yanomamo, sex is central to their mythology as well as their everyday life. Their humor, their insults, their storytelling and most of their beliefs revolve around the theme of sexuality. Men, as almost everywhere, are considered to be superior to women, and their creation myths are

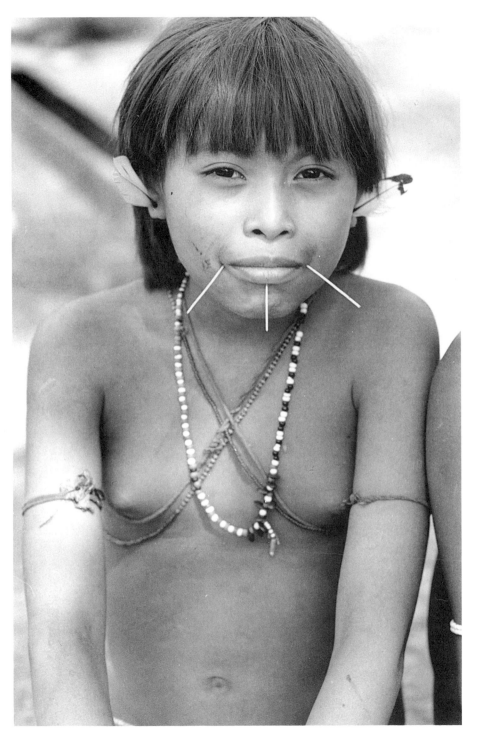

A Yanomami, member of an Amazonian tribe, whose culture is permeated with a distinctly earthy approach to sexuality.

different for each sex. The male myth tells how one of the ancestors shot Moon in the belly. When his blood fell to earth it changed into Men, creatures who were very fierce. Men created in the areas where the blood was thickest fought each other until they were nearly extinct. Now the men needed women to copulate with. One day, when they were collecting vines, a man found a newly opened fruit, called "wabu," which had eyes. Thinking it looked as a woman might, he tossed it to the ground where it changed immediately into a woman and developed a large, hairy vagina. The woman followed the men home. Catching sight of her vagina, they were overcome with lust and each man in turn had intercourse with her. Eventually she produced a number of daughters. As each was born, all the men copulated with the newborn female until there were women in abundance. That, they say is why there are such large numbers of Yanomamo today. Another Yanomamo story, one which illustrates the ubiquitous fear of female sexuality, tells how one of the first beings on earth was a woman. Her vagina turned into a mouth, complete with teeth, which bit off her partner's penis.

What is feared must be controlled. A Yanomamo woman is expected to respond to her husband's needs even before he has told her what he wants. If she is slow to prepare a meal, he has the right to beat her. It is not unusual for a man to inflict serious injuries on his wife, using a machete or an axe, or deliberately burning her. The women accept this treatment and some even see frequent beatings as a mark of their husband's affections. If matters get too bad, however, a woman can usually depend on her brothers to protect her. They have the right to take her away from her violent husband and give her to a more reasonable man. Not until she becomes old does a woman enjoy any kind of respect at all. One result of boys being favored is that they are allowed to prolong their childhood until well into their teens, spending their time playing among themselves. Unusually for native peoples, they have no particular initiation rites to mark the transition into manhood. Girls are kept indoors when they first begin to menstruate and hidden behind a screen made of leaves. They may speak only in whispers and must eat their food with a stick so as to avoid touching it and making it unclean.

Among the Yanomamo as in other parts of the world, Christian missionaries have affected the native attitude toward clothing. For the Yanomamo, nudity is a natural condition; they have no sense that revealing their sexual organs is immoral. Young men may acquire loincloths as a symbol of prestige. Yet where they have been influenced by missionaries, they have accepted a degree of dress. Partly this is because clothing provides a useful protection against mosquitos. They also understand that Westerners find their nakedness objectionable and act accordingly, thus displaying more courtesy than they receive from those who intrude into their territory.

South America: Aztecs, Mayans and Incas

Among the Mayan people of the Yucatan, there was a strict code of sexual morality. Marriage was valued as the most important relationship and extra-marital activity was perceived as a threat to the social order. Adolescent boys were actively discouraged from sexual activity with unmarried women. If caught in the act, a boy would either be fined or, if

Chichen Itza, Mexico. In this ancient ruined city of the Yucatan are to be found remarkable relics of the Mayan civilization.

the girl had been a virgin, he would be forced to marry her. The Maya thought it infinitely preferable for boys to engage in homosexuality until they were able to marry. Parents would provide their son with a slave companion to satisfy his sexual needs rather than run the risk of his finding an unmarried girl for the purpose.

Much more common than sexual misconduct was drunkenness, which was in a manner of speaking the national vice. Local honey was mixed with spices and fermented by being swirled around in the mouths of pretty girls. It was then allowed to ferment and bubble further. Great quantities of this liquor were consumed at religious festivals where it was of the greatest importance that the people should provide the gods with a spectacle of happiness and enjoyment. This, it was firmly believed, would encourage them to send more blessings in the direction of their worshippers. The Mayans were under total subjection to their gods, looking upon them as guides and protectors in all areas of life.

The Spanish conquistadors who arrived in the sixteenth century were horrified by the Mayan acceptance of homosexuality. They immediately assumed that sodomy, abhorrent to the Christian believer, played a major part in all the South American lands they invaded. In relation to the Aztecs, they were on quite the wrong track. Under Aztec law, the death penalty for all homosexuals, whether male or female, was regularly enforced.

The Aztecs had an assortment of earth goddesses and no fewer than five moon goddesses, including Coatlicue, not to be confused with Quetzalcoatl. Coatlicue embodies the cosmic force through which everything potential is solidified into concrete form. According to the myth, nobody knew of her existence for a long time. Lonely and barren, she languished in a cloud. Then the Sun

A decorated skull from about AD 1400. This represents Tezcatlipoca, Aztec God of the Night Sky.

discovered her and took her as his bride whereupon all of her latent powers to create were activated. From then on, it was her power that was the source of the flowering of the seed and the coupling of animals. Coatlicue was often depicted surrounded by skulls, like the Hindu Kali, as a reminder of the necessary rhythm of life and death. It is she who holds the cosmos together and, although more often than not represented as bloodthirsty and warlike, she is necessary for stability and endurance. To her belongs the unsentimental principle of "eat or be eaten." Coatlicue had a son,

Huitzilopochtli, who, like the Greek goddess Athena, was born fully armed. His first act was to kill his sister and his brothers, who had been plotting against their mother.

Perhaps the best-known god of the Aztec pantheon was Quetzalcoatl, a savior god whose mother was a virgin. After the great flood, the myth tells that mankind ceased to exist. The Lady of the Serpent Skirt, an aspect of the Great Goddess, sacrificed Quetzalcoatl and re-created the human race out of blood taken from his penis. One wonders what the Catholic Spaniards made of this story which has echoes of Noah and The Flood and is, in essence, that Quetzalcoatl sacrificed himself, descended into the underworld and was subsequently reborn.

Given the generally ferocious nature of their deities, it is not surprising that the Aztecs were an intensely warlike people. When no obvious conflict presented itself, they would organize a friendly battle with neighboring people. However, their motives for doing so were not altogether harmless. The fact is that the Aztecs needed vast numbers of sacrificial victims. The god they most feared was Tezcatlipoca who, as Sun god, was capable of causing drought and sterility. He was also believed to have stolen Xochiquetzal, the goddess of love and of flowers, from her husband, the rain god. Blood sacrifices were central to his cult, and each year the most handsome prisoner available was chosen to personify him in festivals. At the culmination of the rites, his heart was ripped out of his living body. Because, for the most part, the sacrificial victims were young men, a high birthrate was essential. Early marriage was the norm and divorce and remarriage possible. The Aztecs practiced polygamy, punished those who indulged in non-procreative sex and imposed the death penalty for abortion. Prostitution was, however, condoned and the beauties of the Mexican ladies of pleasure were well-known, if mortifying, to the Spanish priests intent on godly respectability.

The Inca tribe of Peru believed themselves to be the children of the sun, descended from the original Inca family, namely Inti, the Sun and his sister and wife Mama Quilla, the moon and protectress of married women. Many temples were dedicated to the divine pair, the most famous being the Coricancha at Cuzco. In order to preserve the pure line of descent from the Sun, the eldest brother and sister of the ruling family were allowed to marry

Mask of Quetzalcoatl, the plumed serpent God and Aztec savior. c.AD 1400.

nobody but each other, a tradition they had in common with the ancient Egyptians. As with the African peoples, the Incas left no written records. What we know of their culture is derived from the accounts of their Spanish conquerors.

Marriage was seen as the cornerstone of Peruvian society. The ruler, known as the Inca, was considered to be the father of his people and therefore responsible for providing each of his daughters with a husband. Every year a ceremony of mass betrothal was held. Once married, a couple would receive a piece of land and a house furnished by their relatives. Although a man was allowed to have more than one wife, he was not allowed to divorce or replace the principal wife because she had been given to him by the Inca. A widow could remarry only her dead husband's brother. Otherwise she was looked after by her eldest son.

A pottery vessel of a figure wearing a diadem, Moche-style, AD 300-700. Like Greek vases, many of these vessels were decorated with sexually explicit images.

The Inca himself, of course, could only marry his sister, a fellow descendant from the Sun. In addition, however, he had a substantial harem of girls chosen for him at the age of ten and specially educated before being presented to him once they were fifteen. He then chose those he wanted and gave others to men he wished to honor. Those left had no choice but to become Virgins of the Sun, living as nuns and liable to the death penalty if they lost their virginity. When the Spaniards invaded, the Inca attempted to pacify them by bestowing upon them a number of these virgins. Perhaps he expected the conquerors to understand what an immense privilege they were being accorded. It seems doubtful that this was the case.

Despite the invaders' opinions to the contrary, sodomy was regarded by the Incas as something so unspeakably vile that anyone found guilty of the practice was hanged and then burned. So ruthlessly was this penalty enforced that in at least one area there was an enormous excess of women. On the other hand, in part of what is now Ecuador, long before the Conquest, sodomy was reputed to have been practiced quite openly in public. This somewhat unusual custom was based on a legend that male giants had long ago landed on the coast of the area. Because the local Indian women were far too small to accommodate their huge penises, the giants took to practicing sodomy and did so quite openly, in full public view.

The healthy interest which the Peruvians evidently took in sex is depicted in a collection of ceramic drinking vessels from the Moche civilization of the early years AD. These depict a variety of sexual positions, including oral, genital, and anal intercourse. The spouts of some of these pots are shaped like a penis or vulva from which to drink.

Three Tahitians, 1899. Paul Gauguin, 1848-1903 Frustrated by his failure to make a living as an artist Gauguin fled the constrictions of Western civilization to seek happiness in the South Pacific.

Polynesian Paradise?

Hawaii! Tahiti! Samoa! To the average Western imagination these names conjure up pictures of uninhibited sexual frolics, hip-swaying girls offering garlands and sensual delights, an erotic free-for-all with no strings attached.

Perhaps surprisingly, there is a fair degree of accuracy in this colorful image. Captain Cook's traveling companion, Hawksworth, tells how in Tahiti "... young men and girls often copulate publicly before the people, receiving good advice from the bystanders, usually women, amongst whom the most important inhabitants are to be found. Thus the girls (of eleven years) receive their information at an early age." The painter Gauguin, in his book *Noa Noa*, tells how any woman would not hesitate to give herself to a stranger she found attractive. In her eyes this did not mean that a relationship was to follow. On the contrary, she remained independent of the man and was not necessarily interested in making the relationship permanent. In that she remained mistress of herself, she resembled the temple priestesses of the ancient world.

This is not, however, the whole picture. By no means was all sexual activity in the South Pacific consensual. Even today, very different rules apply to men and women and there is a high incidence of rape. Certain customs that are the norm in Samoa would cause an outcry in Western society. It is also interesting to find an ancient Polynesian myth indicating the all-too-familiar masculine fear of the devouring feminine. The savior-god Maui attempted to find eternal life by crawling into the mouth of his mother, Hina. Since "mouth" here could also be interpreted as "vagina," Maui was effectively trying to return to the womb of his Creatress-Mother. Her response was to bite him in two, whereupon he died.

Fundamental to the Polynesian attitude to sexual matters is the nature of their creation myth, according to which all the gods were born from the sexual union between the male Sky and the female Earth. All of the gods from this union were male. To create a human life, a god would take some earth and fashion from it a female form. Having breathed life into his creation, he would promptly mate with her. The result of this curious union, according to the myth, is a human being.

The ongoing effect of this myth was to instill deep into the Polynesian psyche the conviction that creative power, the energy which the Western world calls libido and Polynesians know as "mana," is essentially male. According to the myth, the female, although necessary as a receptacle, has no status or power in her own right. The result, as it manifests in the social order, is that a girl is thought of as belonging to her father and brothers until she marries, at which point she becomes the property of her husband.

In times gone by, the Pacific islanders believed that it was the gods who were responsible for the fertility of the land. Therefore the more their divine libido was aroused, the more productive the earth would be. Religious rituals, as a result, would focus on erotic chanting and dancing, while at harvest time, sexual orgies were held in order to maximize the divine fecundating power. To this day, Polynesian chiefs are considered to be especially powerful channels for the divine "mana" and, in consequence, to be particularly potent. So much so that in the Marquesas, one euphemism for the penis is "chief." Not unsurprisingly, men in this position are polygynous, expected to have many affairs and to father more children than ordinary men. Elaborate rites may be conducted in celebration of the first mating of a chief and possibly the birth of his first child.

Chiefs naturally have special social status but throughout Polynesia unmarried youths, too, are actively encouraged to demonstrate their masculine power and virility by having sex with as many girls as possible. It is here that we meet the traditional picture of Polynesia as a paradise of amicable free love. In practice, however, matters are not quite so simple. Unmarried girls, and particularly the daughters of the best Samoan families, are expected to remain virgins until they marry. So how is a young man to win his sexual colors, as he must? The answer, very often, is rape.

Rape is in fact tacitly accepted in the guise of an activity called "sleep crawling." This involves the young man in question stealing into the girl's house by night and having sex with her, the aim being to try and talk her into it through soft words and gentle persuasion. This is in no way out of deference to the girl's feelings, which do not enter into consideration. It is merely a practical ploy to prevent her from screaming and waking up the family. For a boy who succeeds in his quest, the ensuing kudos come from the fact that he has managed to "steal" sex with an unmarried girl. Whether or not he is really interested in her is irrelevant. What matters most, according to the Samoan scale of values, is that he has managed to steal her sexuality from the men whose family property she is. The youth has thus proved his potency and thereby gained social credibility.

Although "sleep crawling" is an essential activity for any self-respecting Polynesian adolescent, the object of his attentions may well not be a virgin unless she comes from a leading family, in which case she will be strictly watched. Far greater status is awarded to the youth who succeeds in deflowering a virgin. Great rivalry exists among the young men as to who can boast the greatest number of achievements in this regard. Again, this has less to do with actually conquering the girl than with the sport of taking something which is considered to belong to the men in her family. The greatest accolade of all goes to he who manages not only to deflower but also to elope with the daughter of a chief.

CHAPTER 3

Sex in Ancient Civilizations

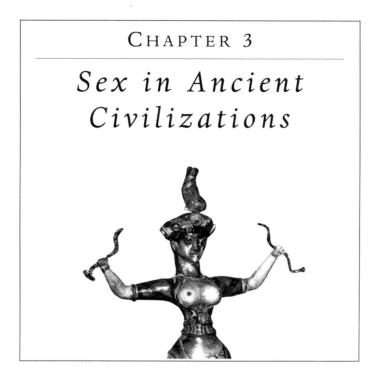

Sumeria: The Earliest Records

MYTH, RITUAL AND SEXUALITY were almost inseparable in ancient Mesopotamia. The earliest deity, the creator-goddess Nammu, meaning "the sea," was believed to have been responsible for creation by giving birth to both heaven and earth. In a later era, the myth changed. Nammu was supplanted by the hero god Marduk who, having killed her, cut her down the middle and used half of her body to make the sky. The more familiar, and historically far more widespread, myth of a masculine god as the supreme creator of the world was now in place. Although it is impossible to account definitively for this development, it was probably the result of invasions of hostile tribes whose values were predominantly masculine into the areas populated by the early, settled, goddess-worshipping people.

Such was the importance of the gods in early Sumerian times that what was considered morally right was for the people almost wholly identified with what was ritually correct. For instance, it seems that the gods were

OPPOSITE: The Temple at Luxor. Fertility god-men worshipped by Alexander the Great, who conquered Thebes in 335 BC and spared only the temples.

quite indifferent to the fact that widows and orphans fared very badly and suffered oppression. Yet they were in the habit of becoming very angry if their worshippers ate ritually impure food. The entire Sumerian culture which dates back to about 5000 BC, was largely underpinned by ritual, much of it explicitly sexual in nature.

The Sumerians were the first literate people, and their written remains provide a glimpse into their world view. Some of the clay tablets, fragments and seals which they inscribed exist to this day, to tell fascinating stories, including the fragmentary story of Inanna. Of all the deities, most of whom were personifications of various aspects of nature, Inanna was the most revered for a long period. Hers was the realm of love and procreation, in which she was a forerunner of Anath of Canaan, Isis of Egypt, and the Babylonian goddess, Ishtar, with whom she is sometimes identified. Inanna herself, it is clear, rejoiced in her sexuality. The story tells how, "When she leaned back against the apple tree, her vulva was wondrous to behold." She herself speaks of making love with her consort, the shepherd Dumuzi, in rhapsodic terms:

> *"He shaped my loins with his fair hands,*
> *The shepherd Dumuzi filled my lap with cream and milk,*
> *He stroked my pubic hair,*
> *He watered my womb.*
> *He laid his hands on my holy vulva.*
> *He caressed me on the bed."*

She addresses him tenderly as "dear to my heart" and "honeysweet" and is explicit in her desire:

> *"Bridegroom, let me caress you,*
> *My precious caress is more savory than honey,*
> *In the bedchamber, honey filled,*
> *Let us enjoy your goodly beauty,*
> *Lion, let me caress you,*
> *My precious caress is more savory than honey"*

Some experts believe that the references to "honey" may well be the origin of our "honeymoon" or "honey month."

The sexual union of Inanna and Dumuzi was the prototype of the Sumerian custom of the "sacred marriage," which was ritually performed at

the New Year festival. This rite later became widespread in other societies, notably Babylon and Greece. In its Sumerian form, the high priestess, known as the "Entu," in order to ensure the renewal of fertility throughout the land, would ceremonially mate with the high priest or king, who personified the life force of the earth. In fact, as far as we can tell, the kings of Sumeria may literally have been sons, fathers and consorts of the high priestesses. As the representative of the goddess the priestess would, through sexual union with the king, bestow her divine power upon him, thereby making him fit to rule. In the ceremony itself, it fell to the priestess to take the initiative and grant her heavenly favors, thereby furthering life. For his part the god-king had to bring her offerings and await her pleasure: ultimate power was in her keeping. Any child born of such a union was considered to be half-human and half-divine.

Further fragments of the Inanna story emphasize the importance to the people of this ceremony. It was the successful performance of the sacred marriage that guaranteed the renewed growth of all human, animal and plant life:

"The people of Sumer assemble in the palace,
The house which guides the land.
In order to care for the life of all the lands,
The exact first day of the month is closely examined...
So that the New Year's Day, the day of rites,

The Seal of the Scribe Adda.
An Akkadian cylinder seal impression from c.2400-2200 BC showing a New Year creation ritual. From left to right are shown Nimurta (with bow), the winged Ishtar, Ea the water god and Shamaash, the god of the sun.

May be properly determined,
And a sleeping place be set up for Inanna."

Inanna is often depicted resting her foot on the back of a lion, offering the king the symbolic objects indicating his ruling power. Lions, when associated with feminine deities, represent the undomesticated, fierce, aggressive aspect of the female. Often such goddesses incorporate a dual nature, the other side of their character manifesting compassion and gentleness. The Buddhist deity Tara is another example. Although primarily benevolent and merciful she is often represented as a fierce, warlike goddess. But it is precisely because of her lion-like power that she is able to confront dangerous forces and this gives her the ability to protect her followers from suffering.

From other tablets we learn that the Sumerians, by present-day Western standards at least, had very little modesty about sex. In the context of the myth of Inanna, with its delight in the erotic encounter, this comes as no surprise. The signs or hieroglyphs representing male and female were simplified drawings of the sexual parts whilst a married person was signified by the juxtaposition of the two. Incantations make it clear that masturbation, alone or with a partner, was a popular technique for enhancing potency. This attitude is about as far removed as it could be from the much later myth prevalent in Victorian times which, as we shall see, considered the practice more likely to drive its proponent insane. Often a man could achieve an erection only by rubbing his penis, or having it rubbed, with a special mixture of oil known as puru-oil. It seems likely that this special oil was mixed with pulverized magnetic iron ore and pulverized iron, no doubt to provide additional friction so as to be more stimulating.

Anal intercourse was practiced and there is no evidence to suggest that it was considered taboo. The "Entu-priestesses" allowed such intercourse during sexual rites in the temples if they wished to avoid pregnancy. Other tablets report homosexual anal intercourse. Both sexual intercourse and prostitution were believed to form part of the divine laws which had governed the universe from the days of its creation and were known to the Sumerians as *me*.

The importance ascribed to the goddess was reflected in the position enjoyed by women within society. Early in Sumerian times, as would happen later in both early Egypt and Crete, women were not confined to

The Sumerian hero
Gilgamesh holding a lion,
symbol of ruling power.
Assyrian stone relief,
Khorsabad, 750 BC.

the home but instead had a role to play in public life. This was especially true of the priestesses, who owned property and transacted business. Property from family estates was inherited equally by sisters and brothers. A daughter, when she married, was given a dowry that she was allowed to keep in the event of a divorce.

Sometime around 2300 BC, all this began to change. The laws inscribed on the tablets changed and, as the status of women deteriorated, their menfolk took a more authoritarian role. A woman might still own property but it was no longer hers to dispose of freely. Now she must first consult her husband and obtain his permission. This would have been unthinkable during the time when the worship of Inanna as giver and supporter of life was paramount and women, as her representatives, were therefore accorded respect and social position. It can be no coincidence that by this later stage, both Inanna and other female Sumerian deities had lost the high position they once enjoyed.

A Sumerian cylinder seal impression from the Ur III period, c.2100-2000 BC. The goddess Ishtar introduces the governor of Akkad to Ur-Nammu, King of Ur, who took the name of the goddess of the primordial ocean, Nammu.

By the time of the Code of Hammurabi, formulated between 1792 and 1750 BC, the position of women had obviously been greatly eroded. The crimes recorded on the tablets which now outnumbered all others were those of witchcraft and female adultery. According to the Code the accused woman was subjected to the ordeal of the river. If she survived being thrown into a river, she was absolved from any crime. Were she to drown, however, this was considered to be proof of her guilt. This way of ascertaining her guilt or otherwise had a continuing influence for hundreds of years. In Europe, women accused of witchcraft were subjected to similar ordeals by water up until medieval times.

From a much later period comes another myth, the Sumero-Babylonian *Epic of Gilgamesh*, which examines the question of why man must suffer and die. Central to the story is the close friendship of its two heroes, Gilgamesh and Enkidu. Although it is impossible to know with any certainty whether their relationship was homosexual, erotic feelings are certainly implied.

Gilgamesh has a dream in which he foresees the arrival of a strange being whom he will embrace "like a wife," and soon after he meets Enkidu and becomes his friend.

Later they meet the goddess Ishtar, who offers to marry Gilgamesh, promising him untold delights. He, however, preferring his friend Enkidu, rejects her advances in a deeply insulting way, referring to her in derogatory terms:

"Thou art but a brazier which goes out in the cold:
A back door which does not keep out blast and windstorm;
A palace which crushes the valiant..."

Enraged, Ishtar asks her father to create a heavenly bull to destroy the insolent hero. Gilgamesh and Enkidu kill the bull and Enkidu throws its organs into Ishtar's face. This is too much for the assembly of the gods, who decide that Enkidu must die. This will be the punishment that Gilgamesh must bear. Later, Enkidu is allowed to emerge from the underworld for a visit and Gilgamesh begs him to reveal what death is like. Enkidu's answer, reluctantly given, implies the former existence of a physical relationship between them:

"That which you cherished, that which you caressed, and which brought happiness
to your heart, like an old garment is now devoured by the worms.
That which you cherished, that which you caressed and which made your heart
glad, is today covered in dust."

Given that myths tend to reflect aspects of the culture prevalent at the time, we may surmise that intimate relationships between men were not considered unusual. This could perhaps be expected in a society where archaeological evidence has shown that women had, by now, a very inferior role. Dual standards existed for married life, where a wife might be put to death for adultery, while a husband was free to enjoy as many women as he chose, provided he did not seduce the wife of another man.

Patriarchal values were indeed increasing in importance at this time, especially in the northern area of Sumeria known as Akkadia, later called Babylonia. This region was inhabited by Semitic tribes in whose view a woman was entirely the possession of her menfolk. So much was this the case that fathers and husbands had the power of life and death over their wives and daughters. The birth of a son was counted as a blessing but an unwelcome daughter might be left, exposed, to die. Not only was a daughter unable to inherit property but she could with impunity be sold into slavery by the men responsible for her. Needless to say, these peoples had no priestesses. As we shall see, this attitude that devalued women had great significance in the later development of Judaism.

Babylon: Home of Sacred Prostitution

OPPOSITE: *Woman at the Window.* The goddess Ishtar depicted as the sacred prostitute, vehicle of the power of feminine sexuality. Megiddo ivory, 8th-9th century BC.

Often associated with the Sumerian goddess Inanna and sometimes interchangeable with her was Ishtar, the great goddess of Babylon, who had two main functions. Although the goddess of love and sexuality, she was in another aspect a fierce war goddess, sometimes depicted riding on a lion. Also called Mother of Harlots and the Great Whore of Babylon, she declared of herself, "...a prostitute compassionate am I." Her holy city of Erech was known as "the town of the sacred courtesans." In no way, therefore, was prostitution in the Babylonian era considered a shameful profession. On the contrary, temples to Ishtar were inhabited by sacred prostitutes or priestesses known as *ishtaritu* or Joy-Maidens, dedicated to the service of the goddess. Their sexuality was seen as belonging to her, to be used therefore only in the sacred rites undertaken in her worship. Indeed, the original meaning of the word "prostitute" was "to stand on behalf of," that is, to represent, the power of the goddess. Curiously perhaps, from a contemporary standpoint, Ishtar was often referred to as "Virgin," implying that her creativity and power were self-engendered and not dependent upon a masculine power.

Forbidden to marry in the ordinary sense of the word, the *ishtaritu* undertook instead the practice of the sacred marriage. Central to this rite was the idea that divine energy was released at the moment of sexual union, where masculine phallic power was received into the feminine embrace. Like Inanna, Ishtar was considered responsible for the power of sexuality and its manifestations. A saying attributed to her makes this clear, "I turn the male to the female. I am she who adorneth the male for the female; I am she who adorneth the female for the male."

Sexuality, as the vehicle by which life both physical and psychic was brought into the world, was considered to be a sacred act. What is more, gods and goddesses, as we have seen in the story of Inanna, were believed to enjoy blissful sexual relationships. Human beings, therefore, through

sexual intercourse might attain something akin to the state of divine ecstasy. In some temples, only a priest would be allowed to represent the Moon God, symbol of masculine divinity. He would have intercourse with the *ishtaritu* or another woman whose role was to embody the feminine power of the goddess. Sometimes the woman in question would be one wishing to be initiated into the mysteries of the Great Goddess. She would accordingly sacrifice her virginity in the temple by enacting the sacred marriage, often with the priest but at other times with a representation of the divine phallus. Perhaps the much later custom of *droit de seigneur*, the right of a feudal lord to have sexual relations with a vassal's bride on her wedding night, was an echo, albeit much distorted, of these ancient religious practices. Some priests, however, although holding office in the temple, would be unable to perform the rite on account of having been castrated. Their devotion to the goddess was such that they had sacrificed their sexuality to her as a way of promoting new life. This practice was later taken up by the Canaanites and in Greece by the priests of Cybele.

What gave the rite of sacred marriage its spiritual significance was its impersonal nature. Those taking the roles of priest and priestess were acting not as man and woman in a human relationship but as incarnations of a divine being. In this way, the participants could expect to have a direct experience of the power of the Great Goddess and feel deeply enriched and energized as a result. Any child born of the union would, as in Sumerian custom, belong to the temple.

In many temples, the priestesses would undertake the sacred marriage with any male worshipper who wanted union with the goddess. The man, whom the priestess had not met before and would not meet again, spent the night with her in the temple precincts. Their intercourse would put him in contact with the rejuvenating energy of the Goddess, mediated through her priestess who would bestow on him an ecstatic experience. For the priestess, the sexual act represented a ritual offering to the goddess. A very real benefit was therefore enjoyed by all concerned, not least the temple itself which could expect to earn considerable income from such worshippers. As

a result, priestesses often engaged in commerce and might be involved in import and export, land management, and other profitable endeavors. The modern brothel of our own culture, with its "madam," might perhaps be seen as a somewhat pale reflection of the temple of Ishtar.

Apart from their sexual and commercial activities, temple prostitutes demonstrated considerable gifts in other areas. Because their natural secretions were considered to have a beneficial effect, they were greatly respected as healers of the sick. One clay tablet dating from this era tells us that diseases of the eye can be cured by a harlot's spittle. These women also acted as seers and were skilled in sorcery and prophecy.

The Jewel of King Osorkon, 22nd Dynasty, 950 BC. This shows the goddess Isis with her brother-consort Osiris and their child, the falcon-headed solar god Horus.

The sacred priestesses were not alone in undertaking sexual rites in the temple. Any number of other women, including those from the highest families in the land, would also prostitute themselves in the temple at least once during their lifetime. Indeed, there was at one stage a law which required a woman to do so before she married. This was a precautionary measure to deflect the wrath of the goddess, for she did not hold with monogamy. The Greek historian Herodotus gives us an excellent, if not wholly approving, description of the practice:

> *"The worst Babylonian custom is that which compels every woman of the land once in her life to sit in the temple of love and have... intercourse with some stranger... the men pass and make their choice. It matters not what be the sum of money; the woman will never refuse, for that were a sin, the money being by this act made sacred. After their intercourse she has made herself holy in the sight of the goddess and goes away to her home; and thereafter there is no bribe however great that will get her. So then the women that are tall and fair are soon free to depart, but the uncomely have long to wait because they cannot fulfill the law: for some of them remain for three years or four."*

For a contemporary person such an attitude is very strange indeed. But in its pure form, a deeply spiritual significance was attached to these rites. The goddess, because she presided over fertility, represented the creative power which is an essential aspect of all female beings. By sacrificing her sexuality to the deity, a woman was offering herself as a vehicle for the divine energy. The experience of abandoning herself in this way evidently engendered a sense of spiritual fulfillment which was more important to her than either sensual satisfaction or even human love.

Temples to Ishtar, at Erech and other places, were also served by male prostitutes. They were referred to as men "...whose manhood Ishtar has changed into womanhood." Attitudes toward homosexuality, however, seem to have changed at a later stage of Babylonian culture. The Middle Assyrian Law Tablets, dating back to the twelfth century BC make it clear that some kinds of homosexuality, at least, could lead to castration:

> *"If a seignior lay with his neighbor, when they have prosecuted him and convicted him, they shall lie with him and turn him into a eunuch."*

In a culture which laid great stress on the duty to procreate, to the extent that a woman's barrenness constituted grounds for divorce, we can deduce that any crime for which castration was the punishment must have been considered extremely serious.

As in most civilizations, incest of any form was strictly forbidden:

> *"If a man violates his own mother, it is a capital crime. If a man violates his daughter, it is a capital crime. If a man violates his son, it is a capital crime."*

Life within the temple precincts was, of course, just one aspect, albeit a central one, of Babylonian culture. An ordinary woman did not enjoy the reverence and exalted position ascribed to the sacred prostitute, her legal position being on the whole inferior to that of her menfolk. Nevertheless, a surprisingly wide field of employment was open to her. As early as the third millennium BC there are records of women working as scribes, hairdressers, shopkeepers, spinners, brewers, diviners, and at numerous other occupations. As a wife, a woman was circumscribed by laws definitely favoring her husband. It was quite within his rights to divorce her for being a spendthrift although he could, if he chose, pardon her should she commit adultery. Although a man was allowed only one legal wife, he was at liberty to take concubines if he could afford them. Should the official wife prove unable to bear children, her husband was at liberty to divorce her. Her only alternative, if he would accept it, was to find another woman for her husband who could assume this role.

Egypt

Perhaps nowhere in the ancient world was everyday life so connected to the country's mythology as in Ancient Egypt. Government had come from the gods who had ruled Egypt from the moment of its creation. From the time of the earliest dynasties, the Egyptian king, or Pharaoh, was regarded as the incarnation of divinity. He was the personification of *ma'at*, the rightness or truth of things with which every good Egyptian wished to align himself. Since the Pharaoh enjoyed divine status, everything belonged to him and the law was as he pronounced it to be.

In the very earliest Egyptian mythology the deity ruling over the heavens is, surprisingly, a goddess, Nut. She is usually depicted arching over her husband, Geb, god of the earth, who lies on his back trying to reach her with his erect penis. Later, and perhaps more familiar to us, came the story of Isis and Osiris. This divine pair had intercourse in their mother's womb – the original divine incest – and loved each other from

Grand Entrance to the Temple at Luxor.
From the lithograph by David Roberts, 1796-1864. The great Temple was built in the 14th century BC on part of the site of ancient Thebes, capital of Egypt at the height of its power.

then onwards. Osiris was tricked by Set, his jealous brother, into lying in a chest, which was immediately closed and thrown into the Nile, to float out to sea. Distraught, his beloved wife Isis searched high and low for his body. Although she succeeded in finding it, Set intervened once more and tore it into pieces. Isis managed to retrieve all the pieces except the phallus, which had been eaten by a Nile crab. Undaunted, she used her magical powers to fashion an image of it, which she used to conceive her Divine Child, Horus. She then performed the very first rites of embalmment, thus restoring Osiris to eternal life. Representations of Isis and Horus were later adopted by the early Christians and transformed into the image of the Virgin and Child.

The myth of Isis and Osiris was of tremendous importance to the Egyptians. Each year the death of Osiris was enacted in a public ceremonial during which the representation of the Phallus was carried in solemn procession. Isis was thought of as the Egyptian throne, the hieroglyph for which is her name and the image of which rests upon her head. This same image can be seen in Christianized form on one of the portals of the western front of the great French cathedral of Chartres. The Madonna is represented as the throne upon which the child Jesus sits and blesses the world, of which he is emperor. In Egyptian imagery, the Pharaohs are depicted sitting on the lap of Isis who suckles them from her breast. In this way the kings receive the divine nourishment which gives them the qualities they need in order to be good rulers. When painted red, the hieroglyph for Isis signified both the female genitals and the Gate of Heaven. Amulets in this form were buried with the dead and contained prayers to Isis in order to deify the deceased person with her magic, which was identified with her menstrual blood.

Relief from the Birth House, the Temple of Hathor, Dendera, Egypt. Originally worshipped as the Mother of Gods, Hathor presided over childbirth.

The queens of Egypt were considered to be Isis incarnate and were therefore almost more important in the eyes of the people than the Pharaoh himself. As mother of the Pharaoh, the queen was exceptionally privileged, even among the royal women. Within the royal family, although not necessarily elsewhere, a matrilineal system of inheritance was in place, leading the Pharaohs to refer to themselves as "Rulers from the Womb." This meant that the dowry of the eldest daughter of the Pharaoh by his principal consort, the Queen, was equivalent to the kingdom itself. She therefore enjoyed equal importance with her brother, the eldest son of the same queen and the Pharaoh's heir, which was one reason why it was the custom for them to marry. On occasions a Pharaoh would consolidate his own claim to the throne by marrying his eldest daughter by his principal wife. So great was the power of the heiress to the throne that, on the death of her consort, Queen Hatshepsut, having no full brothers, decided that she had more right to rule than the next heir and proceeded to do so.

The other and best-known reason for the incestuous marriages made within the royal families of Egypt concerned, almost literally, the royal blood. This, the carrier of the divine essence, must not be diluted. Incest itself is normally and almost universally taboo, for very sound reasons involving the evolution of the species. A race or tribe which is inbred may be perfectly suited to the status quo of its own environment but quite unable to adapt to changing conditions. To meet the challenge of progress, marriage with other tribes is necessary for the further development of intellectual and physical abilities. The Pharaohs, however, as god-kings, were considered perfect, and therefore had no need to evolve. It followed, then, that only one of the same blood could possibly be a fit and equal partner. Akhenaten, for instance, married first his mother and then his cousin, Nefertiti. He subsequently took three more wives, the third and last of whom was one of his daughters by Nefertiti.

Even further back in history, among the ancient god-kings, sacred incest between the father-son and mother-bride was in fact the norm. It was customary for the goddess-queen to take a young and virile consort who supplanted the older, current one. The gods in this case were usually depicted in threes, the goddess, her consort, and their son, who would inevitably replace his father, the old king. This tradition was carried on into Egyptian times and the gods Osiris and Amon were referred to as "Husband of thy mother," as a mark of respect although this was not literally true. Indeed, the trinity which appears in the majority of mythologies is that of father, son and goddess, or Holy Spirit. Only in Christianity do all three take the masculine gender.

Divine or not, the Egyptian royals were as prone to suffering the same high rate of infant mortality as ordinary mortals. This meant that the ideal marriage between a full brother and sister could not always be achieved. Often it was the son of a secondary wife or a concubine who married the

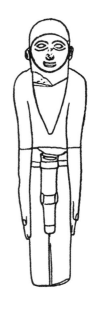

ABOVE: Egyptian statuette showing a non-contraceptive sheath, c.4000 BC.

BELOW: An Egyptian non-contraceptive sheath of the 19th Dynasty, 1350-1200 BC.

Isis suckling the young Pharoah, depicted in the Temple of Hathor, Dendera. By nourishing the king with her divine essence the goddess ensures that he will reign in a manner befitting his exalted position.

king's daughter. Such was the power attributed to the royal blood that Tutankhamun's widow believed that a foreigner who married her could be created Pharaoh, as indeed was to happen.

Outside the exalted circle of the royal family, life in Egypt was more prosaic. For a long period of time, two types of marriage were prevalent and co-existent, old-style matriarchal unions initiated by the wife and terminated only at her instigation, and the more familiar patriarchal marriage. A wife in the latter form of marriage might be little more than a slave, depending on the goodwill or otherwise of her husband. Evidence indicates that wifebeating was not uncommon. Should a woman's husband be convicted of a crime, both she and any children of the marriage had to share his punishment, which usually meant that they became slaves. Unlike other patriarchal societies, property tended to be inherited by daughters rather than sons, along with the responsibility for taking care of aged parents.

In the earliest dynasties the practice of polygamy was fairly widespread, but this gradually gave way to monogamy, except among the royal families. Concubines and slaves were nevertheless part of the picture, as had been the case in Babylon.

Although in Egyptian law, men and women were for all intents and purposes equal, there were few ways for a woman to be economically self-sufficient, unless she were fortunate enough to enjoy a large inheritance. The only professions reported for

Queen Nefertiti, wife of the Pharoah Akhenaten, with whom she initiated many religious and cultural changes. Her astonishing beauty and grace have a timeless appeal.

women are those of dancer and musician, both of which probably involved some degree of prostitution. However, as wealthy households invariably had a large supply of foreign slave girls, and the poor did not marry anyway, it is unlikely that organized prostitution existed on a large scale. In many dynasties it was normal for a woman to make her own choice of lover. A sexual relationship was defined as "knowing a woman perfectly" and a man was enjoined not to be bad-tempered with his mistress. Nor must he attempt to control her. To act in this way toward a woman with whom he had shared a state of ecstasy was considered the height of bad manners.

We know that the Egyptians practiced contraception – in fact, the oldest surviving documents on the subject come from that country during the period 1900-1100 BC. One prescription requires pulverized crocodile dung in fermented mucilage to be combined with honey and sodium carbonate and applied to the vulva. A rather less distasteful and doubtless more effective method involved the use of spongy material to block the cervix, an early forerunner of the modern cervical cap.

Minoan snake goddess from Knossos, Crete, c.1600 BC. According to Cretan myths serpents knew the secret of restoring life to the dead.

Crete: Home of the Goddess and the Bull

Comparatively little is known about the Cretan civilization, which flourished in the third and second centuries BC. The information we have is mainly derived from the innumerable works of art found at Knossos and particularly in the palace of the legendary King Minos, the source of the word "Minoan", also used to describe this culture. Everywhere there is evidence of goddess-worship, particularly that of a snake goddess, a symbol of fertility. From detailed fresco paintings, archaeologists and others have drawn the conclusion that the importance given to the goddess was reflected in the position enjoyed by women. As in early Sumerian and Egyptian times, Cretan women, and priestesses in particular, played a

central role in society. Woman and goddess alike are depicted as elegant and beautiful, wearing jackets which reveal their breasts.

Seals and frescoes depict the sexes enjoying a relationship of equality so that neither sex seems to have dominated the other. Among the famous images of both sexes enjoying activities together are those depicting young men and women, vaulting over the backs of bulls. Although we do not know whether this was part of a religious rite, it is the case that countless representations of the bull and its horns are to be found at Knossos. Since no image of a god from these times has ever yet been found, the bull must have represented the masculine aspect of divinity. Occasionally images of small male figures are to be found in company with the goddess. She may therefore have had a son-lover but such figures are invariably immature, suggesting that the supreme power was hers. The bull has always personified the powerful life force that causes all growth, death and rebirth, for which reason in Egypt it was associated with Osiris. Although in earlier times associated with the moon, it was there connected with the sun as the masculine, creative power of the goddess. As was usual throughout the Near East, a ritual bull sacrifice probably took place each year in order to ensure the continuation of fertility on earth.

The bull-vaulting fresco, Knossos, 1600 BC. In Minoan culture the bull was seen as a sacred manifestation of the life-force.

The Classical World: Greece

Classical Greek culture was inseparable from the myths about the gods of Olympus. Even a brief acquaintance with these tales helps us to understand something of the Greek attitude to sexuality. Zeus, the Great Father, was astonishingly promiscuous, consistently unfaithful to Hera, his long-suffering wife. No female being, goddess, nymph or mortal, was safe from his advances. When necessary, he would resort to taking on animal·form in order to seduce the object of his desire. To seduce Leda, mortal wife of King Tyndareus, he took the form of a swan, in which guise he pursued and made love to her. Among their offspring was Helen, who was subsequently granted immortality. The swan was in fact sacred to Aphrodite, goddess of love and lust. Another story tells how Zeus turned himself into a bull in order to seduce Europa. Nor were his attentions confined to women: his roving eye fell upon the boy Ganymede, whom he had carried up to heaven on an eagle's back. Ganymede was later referred to by the Romans as

Leda and the Swan. Attributed to Nicholas Poussin, 1594-1665. Zeus, ever-artful when sexual conquest was at stake, is here seen disguised as a swan, about to seduce the fair mortal, Leda.

The Temple of Apollo and market place with vaulted building, Corinth.
It is doubtful whether Apollo, who was not known for his sexual excesses, would have approved of the crowds of prostitutes who frequented the city, one of the main ports of Greece.

Catamitus, the origin of our word, catamite, used to denote a boy kept for homosexual purposes.

Perhaps it is this story which serves as a divine blessing on the Greek tradition of pederasty, involving the love of an adult man for a boy in his early- to mid-teens. Pederasty was a widespread phenomenon between the sixth and fourth centuries BC. It became the custom in Athens at this time for a boy who had completed his formal education to be guided by an older man, a kind of mentor and guardian, who would undertake to supervise the boy's further intellectual and moral development. The official line was that this relationship was non-sexual, a pure and altruistic love. To what extent this ideal was maintained we cannot know. Human nature being what it is, it would seem highly improbable, a view supported by Greek writers of the time. While it is true that classical Greece is traditionally associated with homosexual practice, there is little evidence of what exactly was the norm.

We do know that the Greeks were great lovers of beauty and that women were at this period basically held in contempt. A beautiful boy would therefore at the very least be seen as an asset, enhancing the status of the man accompanying him. It is not difficult to imagine that the older man might see in the boy a reflection of his own lost youth and wish to unite with it, thereby gaining at least the illusion of rejuvenation. The boy, for his part, would gain kudos for being the disciple of a distinguished man.

The information we have comes from the works of such writers as Plato and Xenophon. Plato, at least, was firmly of the opinion that the finest type of love was that of the mind, or "platonic love." In his *Republic*, he differentiated between earthly and heavenly love. The former he ascribed to the goddess he calls the "earthly Aphrodite," under whose influence men could be attracted by boys at least as much as by women, and often more so. Heavenly love, on the other hand, he declared to be the gift of a goddess who, by some curious chance, possessed only male qualities. Indeed, she had "nothing of the female" and was "innocent of any hint of lewdness," which would indicate a somewhat convoluted attempt to devalue the feminine and idealize homosexual love.

Unfortunately, Plato's introduction of the idea of dualism between body and soul was to have a profound and devastating effect on the later Christian attitude towards sexuality. Essentially, the body was, in his view, a hindrance to the soul. Because people were so easily enslaved by sensual pleasures, the body, he reasoned, must be a source of evil. Plato's advice to a man seeking truth was to "...cut himself off as much as possible from his eyes and ears and

An amphora from Atticus showing uninhibited Bacchic revels.

virtually all the rest of his body as an impediment which by its presence prevents the soul from attaining to truth and clear thinking."

Subsequent Greek philosophers developed this essentially pessimistic view of the world which, almost by definition, involved a poor opinion both of women and the state of matrimony. In the fourth century BC Diogenes founded the cult known as the Cynics whose devotees rejected worldly comforts including family life. Another group, the Epicureans, who actively pursued "...the sweet things of life," sought to do this by escaping from the world. Their leader, Epicurus, lived in a retreat where people of all classes could come to enjoy a simple life, abstaining from both flesh and wine. His view of sexual love was bleak: "...the physical union of the sexes never did good; it is much if it does not do harm."

While it is true that the Greeks set great store by the intellect, there was also an undoubted emphasis on the physical. An Athenian youth would attend the gymnasia for a sociable workout. This might involve wrestling, running and throwing the discus or javelin, all of which were normally performed naked, after first oiling the body. We might then justifiably

The Birth of Venus, from the Ludovisi Throne. The goddess is helped from the sea by two of her celestial nymphs known as the *horae.* Marble relief, c.470-460 BC.

suppose that the ideal of the non-physical love of a man for a young boy might not always correspond to the practical reality. Greek art, particularly paintings on vases, is the source of much of the evidence for the widespread nature of homosexual relationships. Often, it is two adult men who are depicted practicing anal intercourse. Other paintings, however, show an older man placing his penis between the thighs of a younger.

Boys certainly worked as prostitutes in Athens. Some would walk the streets wearing women's clothes and make-up, although this was generally considered to be beyond the pale and therefore not admired. Laws gradually came into being concerning the relationship between a man and a boy. Around 500 BC, Solon proclaimed that it was illegal for a slave and a freeborn boy to maintain a friendship. Any man who tried to act as pimp for a boy would be deprived of his rights as a citizen, a very harsh punishment in a society where such rights were jealously guarded. An even worse punishment awaited a man who entered the premises of a school without the necessary authority: he risked incurring the death penalty.

Athenian women, as was usual throughout the ancient world, were under the authority of their fathers or husbands. They received no education, had marriages arranged for them and had to spend most of their time in the women's quarters of their houses. Outside the home, a woman would be chaperoned. A wife was not expected to be of higher social status than her husband, and the philosopher Aristotle felt that a husband should be more than twice as old as his wife so that he could dominate her. A man might divorce his wife on any pretext, whereas it was almost unheard-of for a woman to be freed from the marriage bond in this way. Even adultery or pederasty on the part of her husband did not give her grounds for divorce.

Like their Babylonian and Hebrew counterparts, Greek women had no political or legal rights worth speaking of. Indeed, a woman's status was adequately summed up in the Greek word for "woman," namely *gyne*, meaning a bearer of children. A man, it seems, would marry out of necessity but give his affections to a youth. The poet Hesiod pointed out that a man, by enduring the miseries of marriage, would at least have children to support him in his old age. He seems not to have considered that marriage must be at least as disagreeable for a woman. The poet Aristophanes seems to have been more sympathetic to the female cause. In his play *Lysistrata*, he has the women hold a mass sex strike, withholding conjugal rights from their husbands in an effort to force them to put an end to the current war.

In very ancient Greek times, the feminine had enjoyed a more revered place in mythology. Rites involving symbolic death and rebirth were linked with baptism in the waters of the river Styx. This underworld river, across which all souls had to pass after death, was considered to be the bloodstream from the earth's vagina and its waters therefore to have the same dread powers as menstrual blood. In the same way that men swore binding oaths by the blood of their mothers, the gods did so by the blood of the Styx. The place where the river was thought to emerge was marked by a shrine near the city of Clitor, or Kleitoris, which was sacred to the Great Mother.

Curiously enough, the presiding spirit of Athens was a feminine deity, Athene. A virgin goddess, she was worshipped at her shrine, the Parthenon, as Athene Parthenia, or Virgin Athene. According to myth, she was born from the head of her father, Zeus, who had previously swallowed Metis, her mother. Fully grown at birth and clad in armor, she became the protector of heroes as well as guardian of Athens, keeping it safe from enemy attack. Exactly how a city dominated by men and masculine values acquired a female patroness remains a mystery. It is true that in the early years after the foundation of Athens, the Parthenon was served by sacred prostitutes known as "virgins," both in honor of their goddess and because they did not marry. But Athene most definitely did not provide a model of feminine behavior for the ordinary women of her city.

On the contrary, the Greek woman was expected to be a model housewife, running her home and servants, managing the family budget

Dionysus sails across the wine-dark sea with dolphins. From the inside of a cup painted by Exckias, 530 BC. Dionysus is often depicted as a seafarer. Here a splendid vine grows over his boat.

wisely, and being competent in the household arts. Large families did not exist on the whole, probably because marital relations became infrequent once the necessary heirs had been produced. Since wives were forced to be obedient and faithful, they had to provide for their sexual needs as best they could. Help could be obtained from the city of Miletus, which carried on a brisk trade in the manufacture and export of dildoes. Made either of wood or padded leather, they would be lubricated with olive oil before use, either for solitary masturbatory activity or in homosexual practices. The island of Lesbos, home of the poetess Sappho, was reputed to be a center of female homosexuality. Here young women would come to be educated in the mysteries of menstruation and sexuality, eliciting comments from Ovid to the effect that Sappho's work was essentially a course of instruction in female homosexuality.

Sometime during the fourth century BC attitudes began to change. Nude female statues began to appear where previously it had been only the masculine body which was glorified. Women were, in some mysterious way, evidently becoming more interesting to men. The nature of marriage seems not to have undergone a revolution, however, which indicates that wives did not benefit from changing attitudes. Prostitutes, however, benefitted a great deal.

Within the hierarchy of Greek prostitutes, those at the very top of the tree were known as *hetaerae*. They were true courtesans, not only beautiful but also talented and educated, able to entertain men with amusing and well-informed conversation as well as, undoubtedly, sexual expertise. Renowned for their intelligence, they were sought after by men as companions at dinner, a privilege not accorded to wives. Socially, a *hetaera* could do very well for herself, as was the case with Thais of Athens, who became the mistress of Alexander the Great. She subsequently moved even farther up the social scale by marrying Ptolemy I, thus elevating herself to the position of Queen of Egypt. Another world-class *hetaera* was Aspasia, for whom Pericles left his family. Her salon in Athens was patronized by the men who held power. Praxiteles used his lover, the *hetaera* Phryne, as the model for the statue of Aphrodite he created for her temple at Knidos. Phryne was a rich woman and presented to her native city of Thespiai a statue of Eros which Praxiteles had given her.

For a woman who wanted independence, the life of a *hetaera* was infinitely preferable to the domestic servitude which offered the only viable alternative. She was, on the whole, likely to remain unmarried both in order to maintain her equality and to protect her property rights. *Hetaerae* were noted for their shrewdness and the skill with which they managed their finances. They were also remarkably successful at not producing children. How they did so is not recorded, but Greek vase paintings depict courtesans engaged in anal intercourse, a highly effective method of contraception. Above all, they were the only women to play a leading role in the social and intellectual life of the time.

The *hetaerae* formed the very highest class of prostitute, whose lives were worlds apart from those of lesser rank who worked in brothels. Established by, and also paying tax to, the state, these houses of pleasure flourished from the fourth century BC. Their fees were relatively modest although their inhabitants, who would parade their charms on the road outside, were undoubtedly not.

The patroness of all prostitutes was the Olympian deity, Aphrodite. Her temple at Corinth was said to have had more than a thousand prostitutes dedicated to her service. Goddess of love and beauty, she had several titles, each describing a particular function. As Aphrodite Hetaera, she had a temple in Athens where she was depicted sitting on a he-goat. Aphrodite has always been a source of great trouble and even greater fascination to patriarchal society which both desires and fears her as representative of the power of female sexuality. According to legend, Aphrodite was born out of the foam created by the severed genitals of her father, Ouranos, or Heaven, which had been thrown into the sea. Her myth has been celebrated by artists throughout the ages but perhaps most famously by Botticelli in *The Birth of Venus*. Because of her beginnings, Aphrodite ruled specifically over sexual love and lust, being known in this capacity as Aphrodite Porné, origin of our word "pornography."

Like other goddesses of love, Aphrodite also had her terrifying aspect. Her victims would be overcome with frenzied passion, which resulted in tragedy. In Greek mythology her power caused Helen to leave home and follow a stranger, Phaedra to fall in love with her brother, and Ariadne to betray her father. The story of Eros and Psyche tells of Aphrodite's rage that Psyche, a mere human, was adored as a goddess because she was so beautiful. The real goddess therefore sent her son, Eros, to punish the girl, but he fell in love with her instead and became her lover by night, under cover of darkness. Matters went wrong when Psyche tried to steal a look at

Aphrodite of Cnidos, marble statue by Praxiteles, 340 BC. The model for this version of the goddess of love was the artist's mistress the *hetaera*, Phryne.

OPPOSITE: The Temple at
Delphi, Greece, dedicated
to the Apollo but also a
regular setting for the
orgiastic worship of his
brother Dionysus. Delphi
was the home of the
famous oracle of ancient
Greece.

his face, something she had been strictly forbidden to do, as a result of which he left her. Aphrodite then set Psyche four seemingly impossible tasks: sorting a heap of wild seeds into individual grains; snatching a wisp from the fleece of the wild golden rams; drawing icy water from an inaccessible mountain top; and bringing back a casket containing ointment conferring eternal youth and beauty from the underworld. If she could succeed in carrying out these tasks, she would be reunited with Eros. With the help of the ants who sorted the seeds, the reeds and wind who lulled the rams to sleep, the eagle who carried her to the mountain top and Pan who guided her to the underworld, Psyche accomplished each one. Aphrodite still objected to her conduct but finally Zeus interceded on her behalf and Eros and Psyche were united in marriage and had a daughter, Bliss

Although the sexually rich mythology of Greece impinged very little on the average Greek woman's life, some made a connection through their participation in the Great Mysteries of death and rebirth, unknown to this day. Perhaps the most famous were the Eleusinian Mysteries, dedicated to Demeter and Persephone, archetypal mother and daughter. According to the myth, Persephone, an innocent maiden, had been abducted by Hades, ruler of the Underworld and forced to marry him. Demeter, her devoted mother and the Great Mother, mourned to such an extent that earth became barren and no new life was born. The gods, aware that something had to be done, proposed that Persephone return to earth to be with her mother for a part of each year. Unfortunately we do not know exactly what took place during the rites since the initiates were sworn to secrecy and no details were recorded for posterity. There is some evidence that a "hieros gamos" or sacred marriage took place. As in Babylon, this would have involved ritual intercourse between a priest and priestess. The initiates themselves participated in rituals reputed to bring them the experience of being reborn into eternal life. Sophocles gives us a hint of this when he writes, "Thrice happy they be of men who looked upon these rites ere they go to Hades's house; for they alone there have true life."

Slightly more is known about the Dionysian Mysteries. The ever-youthful god of the vine, Dionysus, presided over ecstatic experience and the casting off of inhibition. Carvings show him combining within himself both masculine and feminine elements, for which reason he was referred to by Aeschylus as "the womanly one." A phallic god, worshipped for his sexuality, his was originally a mystery cult for women. His priestess-

followers, known as *Maenads*, would take part in festivals where representations of the god's phallus would be carried in procession. Normally staid and deeply repressed Greek matrons would abandon themselves in rituals involving a display of sexually explicit and even vulgar actions aimed at stimulating the fertilizing power of the god.

Increasingly, the rites developed into events which were decidedly not for the faint-hearted. Worshippers would retreat to wild places in the mountains, as far away from civilization as possible. Here they would feast, drink and dance themselves into a wild and ecstatic state in celebrations known as *orgia*, the origin of our word "orgy." The climax of the festival was marked when they tore apart sacrificial animals with their bare hands and, in an act of communion with the god, ate its raw flesh which represented the body of Dionysus. In earlier times, at a festival known as the *Agrionia*, participants were reputed to have used a young boy as the sacrificial victim. although flagellation later replaced human sacrifice. This is but one of many pagan customs which, as we shall see, the Christian church later borrowed and made its own, albeit in a rather different form.

In due course, the festival came under the control of the state. The rites were now held twice a year at Delphi, home of Dionysus's brother Apollo, and although they continued to be orgiastic, participation was limited to official women representatives from Greek cities.

Rome: Decadence Sets In

The Romans took over the Greek gods, renamed them and absorbed their mythology. Attitudes to sexuality were therefore in many respects parallel to those of the Greeks. Women were, as elsewhere, considered the property of their menfolk. Before becoming a wife, a woman belonged to her father and once married, ownership of her person passed to her husband. The purpose of marriage was, above all, to produce offspring to serve the state and the gods upon whose goodwill the fortunes of the state depended. In her role as mother, a woman enjoyed some degree of dignity, at least during the early Republic. But as a wife she was expected to be subservient. During the first century BC, a woman caught in the act of adultery could legally be killed there and then by her husband. And, even if she confined her excesses to drinking more wine than was considered acceptable, she could be divorced on the grounds of moral laxity.

The Opian Law of 215 BC, marked a watershed in the position of women. They were forbidden to ride in carriages through the streets of Rome, banned from wearing dyed clothes and allowed to keep only half an ounce of gold. Ostensibly designed to help the economy, the law infuriated women more and more until they eventually rebelled. From this time on, they acquired gradually more freedom.

As women, or at least those belonging to the upper classes, gradually became more emancipated, they gained a greater measure of power and control over their lives. Although in earlier years marriage had been marked by ceremonies, sometimes involving proof of consummation, by the third century BC it was defined as a state of living together in mutual consent and could just as easily be reversed. By the end of the first century AD divorce was widespread. From not having been able to divorce at all, a woman could now do so on almost any grounds, including becoming bored with her husband. For his part, a man could decide that his wife was showing her age and divorce her in favor of a younger model. In other words, the Roman attitude to marriage at this time had much in common with contemporary Western views.

Where the important families were concerned, however, matters were not quite so straightforward. Marriage was commonly used in this class of society as a means of forging advantageous political alliances. Under these circumstances, a woman might find herself divorced against her wishes. Roman history is full of examples of the casual dissolution of marriages for this reason. Augustus Caesar, the great-nephew and adopted son of Julius, fell in love with the seventeen-year-old Livia Drusilla and promptly divorced his wife, Scribonia, on the grounds of her moral perversity. His

The Triumph of Bacchus. Scenes from a sarcophagus showing the drunken revels of the god Bacchus, the decadent Roman version of the ecstatic vine-god Dionysus.

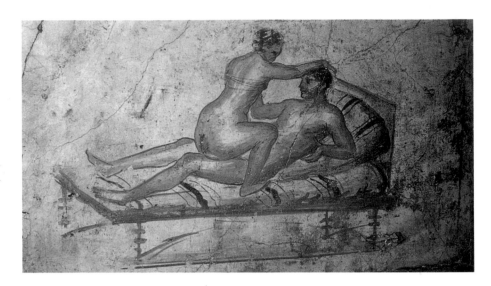

Fresco from the House of the Vettii, Pompeii.
The ancient Graeco-Romans, at ease with their sexuality, were uninhibited about incorporating sexual imagery into their interior decor.

daughter Julia had at various stages two husbands, each of whom was obliged to divorce his current wife in order to marry her.

Things changed drastically when the Emperor Augustus introduced legislation against adultery. Where previously it had been up to the family in question to resolve matters, now the state could step in. Under the new law, a husband had no choice but to divorce an adulterous wife. If he did not, he was liable to prosecution himself. The hapless woman would be further punished by banishment and deprived of half her dowry and a good deal of any other property she might own. Any man so foolish as to think of subsequently marrying her would be committing a criminal offense. The new laws were equally punitive in the case of married men who committed adultery. They too risked being banished. And woe betide any husband whose mistress was not a registered prostitute. He was at risk of prosecution for the crime of unnatural vice. Not surprisingly, there was a rush of applications from many women to be put on the official register as prostitutes following the introduction of this piece of legislation. Among the applicants were the names of many hitherto respectable matrons.

An upper-class Roman woman did not work, certainly was allowed to take no part in public life and had servants and slaves to take care of all her needs. She would while away the hours by taking meticulous care of her appearance, spending money, and meeting friends. Another alternative was to become active in religion. It is small wonder that such women were fervent in their support of the various cults that abounded and whose rites offered some escape from the monotony of the daily routine. Fertility festivals such as the Bacchanalia, the Saturnalia and the Lupercalia provide classic examples of the meeting of mythology and sexuality.

One of the major Roman cults was that of Bacchus. The Greek Dionysus, god of ecstasy and the vine, was adopted by the Romans and renamed Bacchus. He subsequently degenerated into being quite simply the god of drunkenness, around whom a cult was formed. At first this involved a festival which took place three times a year, largely for the benefit of respectable matrons who felt stifled by their lifestyle and needed to let off steam. The proceedings, while often riotous, were nevertheless harmless, a Roman version of the "girls' night out."

As time went on, the nature of the festivities changed. Men were allowed to partake and the festivals came to be held after dark, five times a month. The guiding principle was that all the sexual and emotional restraints of everyday life should be abandoned. Participants would work themselves up into a state of orgiastic frenzy. Women would run screaming down to the

The Feast of the Gods. Hendrik van Balen, the Elder, 1575-1632.

River Tiber to plunge burning torches into the water. Men, high on intoxicants and out of control, would force themselves onto the younger men who were being initiated into the cult. Resistance, under these circumstances, might well mean death. These were indeed fully-fledged Bacchanalian orgies. Matters grew so out of hand that the state eventually had to intervene. Just how widespread the cult had become is evident from the fact that thousands of people were arrested, many from well-known families. Of the men, many were condemned to death. The women were returned to their families, who were required to administer justice in whichever way they saw fit. From that point on, public worship of Bacchus was controlled, it was allowed only to very small groups of people and then only with official permission.

Somewhat less frenzied festivals known as *ludi* or games, were also held in honor of the goddess Cybele, the Great Mother of the Gods and one of the leading deities in Rome. In 204 BC the statue of Cybele was brought from Phrygia to Rome by order of the Cumaean sibyls whose oracles were called upon to guide imperial policy. Her temple stood on the Vatican, on the site of the present-day St. Peter's basilica and survived there until the fourth century AD when it was taken over by Christians. Here she was tended by eunuch priests who would move in a procession through the streets wearing oriental clothes and playing musical instruments. Novice priests wishing to join her order first ceremonially castrated themselves in order to prove their devotion to the Goddess. The operation was carried out using a clamp to hold down the scrotum and testicles which could then be cut off by a single stroke of the knife. In a fertility rite about which little is known, the severed parts would subsequently be buried in the earth.

The eunuch priests were considered to be incarnations of Cybele's son and lover, Attis, who, according to the myth, was about to wed the king's daughter when his mother, who was in love with him, struck him mad. In a fit of madness, or ecstasy, Attis castrated himself before the Great Goddess. A festival was held annually, on the 24th of March to celebrate Cybele's love for her son. On the third day of the festival, known as the *Dies Sanguinis*, the singing and wailing which expressed grief for Attis aroused an orgy of emotional abandonment. In a religious frenzy, young men would wound themselves with knives, some even castrating themselves in front of the statue of the goddess. Other ran wildly through the streets, flinging their severed organs into whatever house they happened to pass. The house

was considered to have received a very special blessing and its residents were required to supply the young man, now a priest almost by default, with women's clothes.

The Lupercalian festivals, originally ceremonies of purification for the New Year, were held in the Lupercal grotto. Here the wolf-bitch Lupa was believed to have suckled Romulus and Remus, the founders of Rome. During the proceedings, male goats were sacrificed, young men were touched with their blood, and priests wearing raw goatskins would strike with a strip of goatskin the hands of a woman who wanted to conceive. Then men and women exchanged clothing and indulged in orgiastic sex. The men chose their partners by drawing small pieces of paper on which were written the names of the women present. February, the month in which the festivals were held, was sacred to Juno Februata, the goddess who

A Bacchanalian Dance. An engraving from the painting by Nicholas Poussin in the National Gallery, London. A grinning statue of the god presides over the antics of lecherous nymphs and satyrs.

presided over the fever of love. In Christian times the church, needing to replace the pagan goddess, substituted the figure of St. Valentine, a mythical martyr. In spite of the efforts of the church to change the nature of the festival, it remained dedicated to lovers, with St. Valentine as its patron saint. The love notes with women's names on them were to become the Valentine cards of the present day. Such was the power of the Lupercalia that, even after it had become Christianized, a form of secret sex worship was still involved and this continued into the Middle Ages. In the presence of witnesses, a couple would engage in sexual intercourse said to represent the marriage of Sophia, the spirit of Female Wisdom, with the Redeemer.

A Vestal Virgin. Early Vestals apparently consummated a highly secret "marriage" with the spirit of Rome, represented by a sacred phallus. The priest in charge of the ceremony was known as the Pontifex Maximus.

Virginity, although not a quality particularly revered in Rome, was most definitely required of a woman chosen to be a Vestal Virgin. In the earliest times the Vestals had been harlot-priestesses. Later, however, girls from the noblest Roman families were chosen for the great honor of becoming Vestals when they were about ten years old and were required to remain virgin for the next thirty years or so. They could then stay or leave as they wished, although most apparently preferred to retain the exceptional privileges they enjoyed. The goddess Vesta represented the sacred fire considered to be at the mystical heart of the Roman empire. Her Virgins were dedicated to guarding the perpetual flame on her behalf, a role of outstanding importance. It was therefore considered essential to the well-being of the nation that their virginity be preserved. Those who broke their vows were put to death, originally by whipping, so great was their crime against the State. Later the punishment was modified, if such a word can be used, and the offender, having been whipped, was walled-up alive in a sealed tomb with only a few provisions. The defeat of the Roman army at Cannae in 216 BC was ascribed to Vestals who had gone astray. As a result, two were denounced and condemned to die in this fashion. Whoever had defiled the Vestal was also punished by being whipped to death in the Forum Boarium. The incarceration of the Vestal Tarpeia was, however, interpreted as a consecration rather than a punishment. As a Vestal, she was believed to be a consort of the god of the underworld. Because she had broken her vows, she was being returned to him, to become his holy possession.

Venus was the ruler of harlots, who tended to frequent the Circus Maximus in search of clients whose libido had been aroused by the Games. There were annual festivals to Venus: married women worshipped her on the first day of April, and harlots, both male and female, joined in their official celebration on the 23rd.

Venus was not the only goddess to preside over sexual rites. Aristocratic matrons at the highest level of society would prostitute themselves in the temple of Juno Sospita in the hope of having a revelation. Birth rituals also came within the province of the feminine deities, and the various different kinds of midwives were all connected with the women's temple. The delivery would be performed by the obstetrix while the "nutrix," or nurturer, taught mothers the techniques of nursing. Priestesses of the goddess Ceres, known as the *ceraria*, would perform the requisite birth rituals.

Whatever might be required of the Roman citizens, the imperial households were a law unto themselves. The lives of most of the emperors stand among the worst examples of cruelty and depravity in history. Plotting and planning, sexual or otherwise, was normal. Any woman who strayed from her duty or was the victim of a political plot to remove her might find herself accused of nymphomania, taking part in sex orgies, being an alcoholic, or planning to poison a rival. One has only to read *I, Claudius* by Robert Graves to obtain a graphic picture of the hysteria and dissoluteness rife at court and elsewhere.

Priapus, god of fertility, from a fresco at the House of the Vettii, Pompeii.
Priapus was the son of Aphrodite, goddess of sexual love and Dionysus, god of ecstasy; hardly surprisingly he is usually depicted in a permanent state of erection.

Given that Roman society was essentially masculine and patriarchal, it is curious that women were allowed such a degree of sexual freedom for so long. One obvious reason is that husbands and wives tended to lead completely separate lives. If a man had married a woman for whom he felt no affection, as many certainly did, he may simply have been indifferent to the way in which she occupied herself in his absence. Economic reasons may have also played a not inconsiderable part. A wife would bring with her a dowry, possibly a very large one, and it was therefore in a husband's interest to keep her – and it. The fact that there were in general more men than women must also have entered into the equation.

The original laws of Rome required parents to raise all their male progeny but only the firstborn girl. For a long period, the majority of parents obeyed this law to the letter, not least because a father would in due course be expected to provide a dowry for his daughters. Among the more affluent, this might be a matter of a very considerable sum. The state obligingly made available places in the city where unwanted girl babies, together with deformed or illegitimate boys, could be abandoned. The majority of such infants would be simply left to die from exposure, although some would certainly be taken by strangers to be brought up as slaves. Since this practice continued until the fourth century, a shortage of girls in any one generation created a shortage of mothers for the next. The upper classes thought two sons enough, the traditional "heir and spare," one to inherit and one in reserve in case the first failed to survive. To have more sons would mean breaking up estates in an unacceptable fashion. The professional classes tended to hold similar views.

A couple who did choose to marry would without doubt practice contraception. In the view of the writer Pliny, the most effective method was to find ways to lessen sexual desire. His suggestions as to how to go about this include applying mouse dung in the form of a linament, a method which would indeed be guaranteed to do the trick. On the other hand, his readers were advised to swallow pigeon droppings mixed with oil and wine. Pliny does not tell us whether these remedies were a result of personal experience. Another writer, Dioscorides, recommended the use of pepper as a contraceptive. It was to be inserted into the mouth of the uterus immediately after intercourse. Early in the second century, a gynecologist named Soranus proffered his advice, based on his studies in the city of Alexandria. He recommended plugs for the uterus, made of wool and

Head of Plato, the Greek philosopher, whose ideas about love were to influence the early Christian view of sexuality as a necessary evil.

soaked in a substance such as cedar gum or an astringent solution, which would contract the uterine opening and enable it to fit closely around the plug. If that were not possible then he had a different suggestion. At the moment of the man's ejaculation, the woman should hold her breath and draw back from him before immediately getting up and sitting with her knees bent while doing her best to sneeze. Such activity on her part would prevent the semen from entering the womb.

For the poorer classes, such concerns were immaterial, since they could not afford to marry in any case. The state handout of daily food to the indigent was only just enough for a man, let alone a wife and family. Slaves rarely married since men were in an overwhelming majority in this category. Freedmen were allowed only to marry freedwomen, whose numbers were small. Even if a freedman managed to find a wife, she would probably be approaching the end of her childbearing years, since few were granted their freedom while they were young. The way Roman society was organized was therefore almost guaranteed to ensure a minimal birthrate and this was one fact that contributed to the decline of the Roman Empire.

Priapus in the form of an oil lamp from Pompeii, 1st century AD.

Other factors also played their part in the population decline. The lead which was present in the face powder regularly used by women, as well as in the pipes carrying water, in cooking utensils, and in the winemaking process could easily have contributed to a high incidence of miscarriage and stillbirth, and of sterility in men. Also, the men drank a great deal of alcohol, which we now know has an adverse effect on the levels of testosterone in the body.

The situation eventually became so serious that Augustus created laws to try and remedy matters. Widows had to remarry within two years and divorcees within eighteen months. An unmarried man was not allowed to receive a legacy. Childless couples who were still young enough to conceive were allowed to inherit only half of anything left to them. The rules prohibiting intermarriage between the classes were lifted and all except the upper classes were permitted to marry freed slaves. Special allowances were given to couples who had several living children. But even the best efforts of Augustus could not prevent the eventual decline not only of the population but of Roman society as a whole. What was formerly such a powerful empire was eventually to flounder on the shores of decadence.

CHAPTER 4

The Art of Love

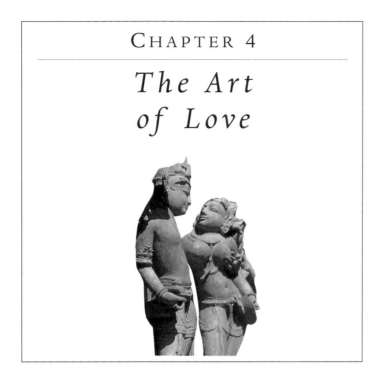

S EX IN WESTERN SOCIETY has been practiced almost exclusively either for the purpose of procreation or in pursuit of pleasure. Once temple prostitution ceased to exist – with the help of the early Church fathers – sexuality and spirituality came to be seen as opposing forces. Only a few Gnostic groups continued to regard sex as a means of spiritual development. In Eastern culture, on the other hand, sex has not only been regarded as natural and beneficial to health, but, for centuries, it has been used as a way of expanding and exploring spirituality. Religions such as Taoism and Tantric Buddhism understand sex as an entirely natural and health-promoting activity. What is natural, joyful and harmonious, they reason cannot be wrong. The only grounds for guilt in respect to sexual activity are if the experience is wasted or in some way debased. The path to spiritual awakening lies within the ecstasy of true sexual fulfillment. Activating the energy currents of the body through sexual experience and physical harmony can be a way to achieve enlightenment and this outlook is common throughout the Far East. In China, it is referred to as "provoking the spirit."

OPPOSITE: The elegant Japanese courtesan, Nakagawa, from the painting by Eishi, 1796.

China and Taoism

To the average Western way of thinking, the idea of sex as a means of achieving spiritual happiness is quite foreign. But in China the Taoists have always thought of it as a way to further one's knowledge of the Universe.

The meaning of the word "Tao" is not easy for a Western mind to grasp since it represents a very different world-view. Loosely translated, it means "The Way" and describes the continuous flow that creates the harmonious balance of the Universe. Taoist philosophy maintains that everything is in a constant state of change as a result of the interplay of the two great forces of the cosmos, "yin" and "yang." All manifestations of life are made up of these two forces, yin being the feminine force, which is passive and receptive in its nature, and yang the masculine, which denotes everything that is active and dynamic.

Within this flow of energy, which permeates all creation, anything can be seen as a vehicle for God's energy and whatever we choose to worship may therefore be thought of as containing the essence of God. The act of sex, viewed in this light, becomes an act of supreme worship. Perhaps this thought is not so very strange to the Western mind when we think of the words of the Christian marriage service "...with my body I thee worship." For the Taoists, however, these words are actually put into practice. Sexual ecstasy is a joining not only of bodies but also of souls. The union of man and woman should be like the harmony of heaven, which is yang in nature, and earth, which is yin.

In the oldest Chinese inscriptions the color red was associated with women, sexuality, and the ability to create. The marriage ceremony was known as the "Red Affair." In these early times white represented both death and sexual weakness. In later erotic and alchemical literature, the woman was referred to as red while the man was white. Women in this belief system, were credited with magical powers and considered to be the teachers of sexual knowledge. Although this early view was largely replaced by the Confucian patriarchal system, which inevitably held the man to be superior, it continues to inform Taoism and Taoist sexual practices to this day. These were based on the view that women have an inexhaustible supply of sexual energy, or life-force, which the man could assimilate during sexual intercourse.

Taoism therefore emphasizes the importance of not changing partners often and avoiding casual sexual encounters. This is based on the belief that when we unite with somebody sexually we exchange energy with them. If they are loving we will take into ourselves some of their love. But if they are unhappy or unhealthy we will absorb that too. Taoist sex is not romantic in the Western sense, in that it is more impersonal, the focus being not so much on feelings as on the experience of a powerful flow of energy, which could be prescribed and regulated by all practitioners.

A man was considered to have a limited supply of yang essence, or semen, while a woman's yin essence was limitless. In order to strengthen his vital energy, a man needed to absorb the female yin essence contained in the vaginal fluids. Enormous importance was attached to intercourse without ejaculation, so that the man might conserve his precious supply of semen. The very best sexual experience was the one whereby the woman was completely satisfied but the man not exhausted. For her part, the woman could have as many orgasms as she wished, the more the merrier in fact, since it was during orgasm that her yin essence was at its very peak. It followed that the more the man could prolong his activities, the more yin essence he would absorb. It was thought that women did not lose energy through orgasm; on the contrary, it helped them to absorb the male energy that was considered beneficial for them. A woman's vital energy or *ch'i* was believed to be receptive and in need of constant recharging from a man's more active energy; without this she might become lethargic and dissatisfied. Equally, a man's *ch'i* needed constantly to be grounded to that of a woman or he would become restless and irritated.

An important feature of Taoist sexual practice is that, for the man, orgasm and ejaculation were seen as quite separate. Ejaculation was for procreation and otherwise not desirable. But a man could have as many orgasms as he wished provided that he retained his vital fluids so that the semen, or *ching*, could flow upwards through the spinal column. Strengthened by the contact with the female yin essence, the *ching* could nourish his brain and therefore his entire system. This practice of restraint resulted in an intense orgasm known as the "Plateau of Delight," in contrast to an orgasm accompanied by ejaculation which was called the "Peak of Ching."

Although a man was to avoid sex with too many strangers, it was thought that sexual intercourse with several regular partners was highly beneficial. The variety of female energies he absorbed would be particularly strengthening. Where polygamy was practiced a man who could afford it would have anywhere from a dozen to perhaps thirty wives. This made it feasible for him to have intercourse with at least ten different women in any one night, a practice believed to increase his strength immeasurably. Where this was the case, it was incumbent upon the husband to make sure that the sexual needs of each of his wives were met. Indeed, a man's fitness for public office would be reflected in the degree to which he succeeded in maintaining domestic harmony under potentially difficult circumstances.

Kissing, touching and caressing were considered an intrinsic part of the daily Taoist sexual rituals, whether or not they led to intercourse. Through mutual loving caresses energy flows through the body. That there is truth in this assertion is perhaps shown in cases documented in the West whereby newborn babies, who have been deprived of physical affection, become emotionally withdrawn and have even been known to die. Taoists believe that whenever we touch another with affection we also do something beneficial for ourselves.

Great emphasis was placed on sensual kissing, which was considered so erotic and private that even to this day the Chinese rarely kiss in public. In former times a woman seen doing so was considered to be acting like a prostitute. Sexual intercourse in public, however, does not seem to have been considered quite such a private affair. In the first centuries AD, public ceremonies of sexual intercourse were known to have taken take place, often at certain phases of the moon. A ceremonial dance would be held, after which members of the assembly would have intercourse in the presence of the others.

Foreplay for a Taoist is a most important aspect of the sexual experience, to be enjoyed for its own sake and not merely, as in the West, as a forerunner to intercourse. It is essential to the practice of good sex that the fluids and secretions be flowing and harmonious. If penetrative sex takes place before a woman's vaginal secretions are flowing and moist it is not only painful for both partners, but it also impedes the exchange of vital essences. Although masturbation has no place in Taoist sex for men, since it offers them no energy in exchange for the precious vital yang essence lost, oral sex was recommended. This was, however, with the proviso that the man did not ejaculate during fellation because the only proper place for semen to be deposited is the vagina. Since women, with their inexhaustible supply of sexual energy, were not believed to lose any during orgasm, there

A 19th century Chinese geomancer's compass, or Pa Kua, on an amuletic board, showing the Yin/Yang symbol which is central to Taoist thought.

TOP: *At the Trot.*
Below: *At the Gallop.*
Agile lovers enjoy sexual
congress on horseback.
From a series of prints
showing scenes from the
lives of Mongol horsemen
in the Tao-kuang period c.
1850.

was no rule against female masturbation. Cunnilingus was very much favored both as an excellent means of preparing the woman and as an aid to the man in imbibing more of her yin essence. Although anal intercourse was allowed, it was not, generally, looked on with favor as it was felt that it would do little to strengthen the man's energy.

Given that sex was of such fundamental importance in Chinese philosophy, it comes as no surprise that they produced what were in fact the world's original sex manuals, highly detailed and illustrated. What is often thought of by Westerners as Oriental pornography were in fact intended as serious reference books, designed to educate the reader how best to achieve the perfect harmony of yin and yang. Great stress was laid on the importance of both partners being in the properly receptive mood. The first Taoist sex techniques were described in the *Yellow Emperor's Classic of Internal Medicine* dating back to around 1500 BC. This work took the view that when a couple practiced sex properly they would stay young and healthy, enjoy increasing strength and vitality and live longer. To waste sexual energy would, on the other hand, lead only to poor health and premature aging. In this view the Taoists were very much at odds with the traditional Buddhists, who favored celibacy and a monastic existence as the best way to live.

In complete contrast to the somewhat clinical Latin names used in the West for the sexual organs, the ancient Chinese terminology is highly poetic. Intercourse itself, as a reflection of the union of heaven and earth, yin and yang, is referred to as "Clouds and Rain," indicating the clouds rising from the land to meet the rain descending from the heavens. Female orgasm is called the "Bursting of the Clouds." The penis is referred to as the "Jade Hammer" or "Jade Stalk" and the vulva as the "Jade Gate" or "Golden Cleft." An erect penis becomes the "Positive Peak" or "Vigorous Peak." The clitoris is referred to variously as the "Jewel Terrace" or the "Pearl on the Jade Step" while the labia are known as the "Examination Hall" and the vagina as the "Cinnabar Gate."

The most natural position for intercourse was considered to be with the man above since that best represented the cosmic image of heaven above earth. However, a large variety of alternative positions included, for instance, "Mandarin Ducks Entwined" where the woman lay on her side, curling her legs to enable the man to enter from the rear. Alternatively, the couple may have been in the mood for "Late Spring Donkey," with the

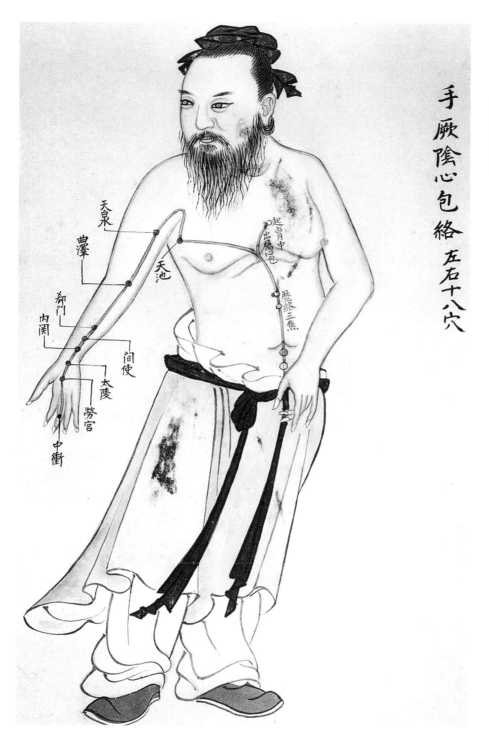

手厥陰心包絡左右十八穴

天泉

曲澤

天池

郄門

內關

間使

太陵

勞宮

中衝

起膏中
出屬心包

歷絡
三焦

An 18th century Chinese drawing showing the series of acupuncture points for controlling diseases of the sexual organs.

Lovers with a Bowl of Flowers, from the painting by Yushido Shunsho, c.1785.

woman bending over, supporting herself on her hands and feet and the man standing behind her holding her waist. Whatever the position favored, it was incumbent upon the man to make love to his partner ecstatically and poetically, a requirement not much highlighted in the equivalent volumes available in the West today.

Great attention was paid to the different types of penile thrusting. Since the aim of coitus was to produce energy, the proper friction was required in order to produce the spark. The seventh-century manual, *T'ung Hsuan Tzu* gives some detailed instruction:

> *"...deep and shallow, slow and swift, direct and slanting thrusts, are by no means all uniform and each has its own distinctive effect and characteristics. A slow thrust should resemble the jerking movement of a carp toying with the hook; a swift thrust that of the flight of the birds against the wind. Inserting and withdrawing, moving upwards and downwards, from left to right, interspaced intervals or in quick succession, and all these should be coordinated."*

A skilled practitioner might at one time "...push in slowly as a snake entering a hole to hibernate" while at another he could "...rise and then plunge low like a huge sailing boat braving the gale." A sequence of nine shallow thrusts followed by a single deep one was especially favored, not least because nine was considered a magical number.

Such high levels of sexual activity inevitably called for mechanical aids, at least for those who were less than expert practitioners of Taoist sex. Aphrodisiacs included a potion made of powdered deer antlers or certain fungi. To help a man maintain his erection, he could fit a ring around the base of his Jade Stalk which would be made of ivory or jade and held in place by a silk band. In order to enlarge the penis, a man could wear a set of small round balls held in place under its skin. The female version, called "tinkling balls," were inserted into the vagina, enabling a woman to bring herself to orgasm simply by making undulating movements of the hips.

Although polygamy was the norm, prostitution nevertheless flourished in China. Brothels were civilized places where a man might go to relax, eat, drink and enjoy entertaining companionship. There was no pressure for him to have sex unless that was what he had in mind. And when he did, the experience could provide a welcome respite from the control he was expected to maintain with the women at home. The yin essence of a

Lovers with Hand to Mouth, from the painting by Yushido Shunso, c.1785. The Japanese have a long tradition of explicit erotic paintings by many of their finest artists.

prostitute, by virtue of the number of clients she served, was thought to be far more powerful than that of an ordinary woman. It was therefore not so critical for the man to avoid ejaculation, since her energy would easily replenish any that he might lose.

The inhabitants of the brothel would range from the highest class of courtesan to the merely ordinary. The girls at the top would be educated and skilled, reminiscent of the *hetaerae* of Greece. A customer was, if he wished, able to buy the girl of his choice to become his concubine or, if she were of the highest rank, his wife. The brothels themselves ranged from the cheap whorehouses catering to the needs of the poor to the top-ranking establishments known as "sing-song houses" or "tea houses." These served the wealthy and the educated classes and were extremely expensive, offering in return the best quality of everything, from furnishings and entertainments to the women themselves.

Although some Taoist ritual was highly esoteric, it was, on another level, the popular religion of the masses, who responded with enthusiasm to the many magical elements it contained. In complete contrast was the patriarchal system of Confucius, a man of reasoned and some might think rigid views, particularly about the conducting of family relationships. Although the Taoist and Confucian philosophies could scarcely have been more different, until the twelfth century people saw nothing odd about adopting a Taoist attitude in private life while understanding Confucianism as the best system of maintaining a stable society. The Confucian view of women was that they must be kept in their place, naturally a lower one than that enjoyed by their menfolk. This extended to the physical layout of a home, which ideally would have separate quarters for the women, thus ensuring that husband and wife would have minimal contact. A woman's duty was to be a good and obedient wife, a producer of healthy, preferably male, children, and a prudent housewife – hardly an original view. It was extremely important for her to bear many sons since to them fell the task of carrying out the honors due to the ancestors, upon whose well-being depended the future happiness of the family.

Confucius has nothing to say about sexual relationships, and so Taoism continued to be practiced by people who otherwise subscribed to the Confucian system of values. Outside the bedchamber a man was expected to show no interest in his wife and certainly no affection. His principal loyalties lay with his parents, and the notion of filial duty was all-important.

It was not unusual for a man to take a concubine. In fact, if a wife were unable to produce a son and heir, she was expected to encourage her husband to do so. Girls from poor families were often sold for this purpose, which could expose them to a life of great unhappiness. If a concubine had been purchased in order to produce a son, and failed to do so, her presence in the household would simply be ignored. From the tenth century onwards, both wives and concubines were exposed to the custom of foot-binding, which continued right up to recent times. A tiny foot was considered the epitome of feminine charm and helplessness. It also ensured the impossibility of independent action on the part of the woman. Little girls would begin to undergo the crippling process of foot-binding from the age of about five when their feet were first bandaged in such a way that the bones were broken and the flesh deformed, often resulting in death through gangrene.

Japan: The Floating World

The old religion of Japan was called *Shinto*, meaning "The Way of the Gods," a term first used by the Chinese to distinguish it from "The Way of the Buddha" which they introduced into Japan. According to the oldest Shinto mythologies, two of the original gods who appeared out of formlessness were the ancestors of the whole of creation. Known as Izanagi and Izanami, they came down to earth by means of thrusting the "Jewel-spear of Heaven" downwards into the ocean, where drops from its point became an island where they built their palace and erected a heavenly pillar. The strong phallic symbolism of this story emphasizes the essentially masculine values which underpin Japanese society and culture. Another influential aspect of the myth is that Izanagi, the god, rebuked his wife for being the first to speak which, he said, was "not proper" for a woman.

The Master Loves the Courtesan (detail), from the painting by Isoda Koryusai, 1750-1800.

Another heavenly pair who occupied a leading place in Japanese mythology were the sun goddess Ama-terasu and the storm god Susa-no-wo. Their continuing struggles depict the battle between light and dark or winter and summer. Perhaps curiously for such a masculine-oriented society, Ama-terasu was the principal deity of Shinto and was thought to be

Portrait of the Floating World, from the painting by Utamaro. The courtesan shown here encouraging her lover would have lived in the area of the city set aside for brothels and tea-houses.

the ancestress of the legendary first Emperor of Japan, Jimmu. In ceremonies reminiscent of Druid and other European fire rituals, special rites were performed each winter to ensure the renewal of the sun's power. The Sun Goddess was perhaps also the original female shaman, or *miko.* Shinto attached great importance to women of this type, if no other, because their powers as mediums allowed them to act as channels for the voices of the gods or ancestors. *Miko* were to be found not only in towns and villages throughout the country but also at the imperial court, where they had the job of transmitting instructions from the gods to the Emperor.

Shinto advocated a full and enjoyable sex life for married couples. To this end, a bride would be given a copy of a sex manual known as *shunga,* or "spring pictures." The pictures in question depict couples engaged in all manner of sexual activities, encompassing almost fifty different positions, together with a wide range of information on topics such as masturbation, aphrodisiacs and sex aids. The explicit nature of the illustrations might

A elegant geisha carefully applies her make-up with a brush, 1825.

seem pornographic to the Western eye, particularly as the couples are often shown with genitalia of exaggerated dimensions. For the Japanese, however, their purpose was not simply to arouse but also to educate.

The phallic gods of Shinto were much in evidence in everyday life. Many of these had the job of staving off demons while others, represented by either phalli or human figures, were set up at the outskirts of villages to ward off disease. Women would tie slips of paper to the large phallic images often to be found by the roadside in the hope of finding a handsome lover. Since the 1868 revolution, successive governments in Japan have attempted to repress the more obviously phallic symbols in temples by draping them with red fabric. As always, however, old customs die hard, and even today bamboo poles are erected outside shops and houses at the time of the New Year.

Some sects of Buddhist monks in Japan, especially the Tachikawa sect, founded in the eleventh century, taught ways of using sexual intercourse as a means of attaining Buddha-hood through one's body. The few surviving texts are translations of Indian Tantric texts and describe Tantric rituals. Illustrations of what is called the "sexual mandala" show a couple lying naked, the man on top of the woman with his head between her feet and her head between his. On the various body parts are marked magical spells. Although the Tachikawa sect was outlawed in the fourteenth century and its books burned, the teaching seems to have survived underground, for there are references to it in the seventeenth century.

From before AD 1000, Taoist sexual manuals were introduced into Japan. The emphasis in these manuals was upon correct mating so as to promote longevity and health, as opposed to the spiritual experience provided by Tantric practices. As in all Taoist texts, particular attention is paid to instructing the man not to ejaculate but rather to build up his strength by exercising self-control.

Since both menstruation and childbirth were considered to be polluting, women in either condition were obliged to live in a hut away from the main building and to take their meals alone. Some Japanese Buddhists monasteries refused to allow women visitors lest they should be menstruating and therefore defile the sanctity of the place. This custom is still met with in parts of India today. Morals were strictly protected and girls, once they were about ten years old, were not allowed to play with boys, in the cities at least. A girl belonging to the Samurai warrior class, who occupied a kind of middle ground between the nobility on the one hand and the merchants and peasants on the other, was given a pocket dagger when she reached maturity and taught how to use it to defend herself should a man try to endanger her chastity. If, in spite of all social precautions, a girl were to become pregnant, either a quick marriage would be arranged or else the girl might be sent away to be a concubine or a geisha after the birth of the baby.

Homosexuality was prevalent in the warrior class. Shrines and even Buddhist temples were frequented by homosexuals. The emphasis on men was highlighted in the traditions of the No and the Kabuki theatre, where women are to this day forbidden to work as actors, so that the men must take female parts, sometimes continuing to act as women offstage as well.

Erotic painting has been developed in Japan over the centuries. A thirteenth-century scroll depicts a courtier and his lady performing sexual intercourse in sixteen different positions. Before the seventeenth century, paintings show women with full breasts, ample hips and slender waists, emphasising their fertility and sexuality. Men appear with strong bodies and thick beards, emphasizing their virility. Later, however, the Japanese followed the Chinese lead in changing their ideas of beauty, going to the other extreme, depicting very frail looks and classic oval faces.

One of the best-known painters of the late eighteenth century was Utamaro. His work features not only the daughters of the wealthy, from whom he presumably derived his income, but also courtesans and more lowly prostitutes. Pictures of prostitutes who plied their trade from unlicensed teahouses clearly show that such women were regarded as simply the playthings of men. These women were thought at the time to have an altogether lower level of existence, devoid of spirituality, and were therefore considered by orthodox religion to be sinful and polluted.

The authority in Japanese family life lay firmly with the men. Marriage in Japan, until very recent times, was an arrangement between the two families concerned and orchestrated by go-betweens. Gifts were exchanged, special clothing worn for the occasion and a wedding-feast held, after which the union might be consummated in a nuptial hut. Once married, the role of the Japanese woman was to serve her husband in all ways and to bear his children. Peasant women were more fortunate in that they enjoyed more freedom of expression than elsewhere in society and could have a relationship of some degree of equality with their husbands. This was

Portrait of the Floating World, A Pair of Lovers, by the famous Japanese artist, Utamaro. The courtesan uses a dildo strapped to her leg while her lover looks on. From *The Poem of the Pillow.*

unthinkable for well-bred women of the middle and upper classes, who were required to be submissive and repressed, appearing only when needed, otherwise fading into the background. Since this hardly made them the most stimulating of companions, men sought more entertaining female company outside the home. A man of the upper classes might have the resources to afford a mistress or perhaps a concubine or two. For a middle-class man there were prostitutes and geishas.

These ladies of pleasure were to be found in the areas of major cities which were specifically devoted to such pursuits, known as "The Floating World." Because it was considered perfectly acceptable and not in the least shameful for a man to visit a courtesan, the brothel area was a pleasant place with cherry trees and well-lit streets, a far cry from the tawdry red-light districts of some modern cities. When Tokyo was in the planning stages, a designated area for courtesans was specifically set aside. By the middle of the eighteenth century it boasted some three thousand inhabitants, elegant and richly clad in beautiful kimonos. There was no question of the prospective customer picking up a girl off the street. He had to make an appointment through one of the tea-houses.

Some of these tea-houses provided entertainment by highly-trained dancers, singers and musicians of both sexes known as geishas. Contrary to popular belief, they were not prostitutes although their dancing and singing was suggestive, expressing in words and movement things which a wife could not. However, the term was sometimes applied to a woman who was either a courtesan or even a prostitute. True geishas demanded and received great respect. If a man wanted sexual intercourse with a geisha and it was allowed, she would formally have to become his mistress, at least for a time. Even in today's rapidly changing and, in Japan, ever more Westernized society, geishas are still to be found. Often they come from rural areas, the daughters of poor people who have sold them for the purpose.

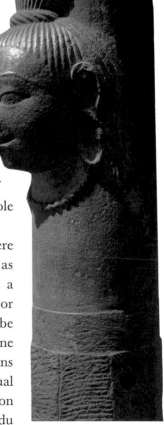

This lingam, the phallic figure of the god Shiva, has one of his five faces carved on top. The lingam is the main object of worship in Saivite temples and private family shrines.

India: Home of the Love Deities

Nowhere more than in India have mythology and sexuality been so intimately connected. Hindu divinities come in pairs, often eternally conjoined in blissful sexual embrace. Unlike most Western religions, Hinduism has never been concerned with suppressing sensuous pleasure. Body and spirit are considered an integral whole, never separated with prejudice in favor of the spirit as was the case with Western dualism. Rather than attempting to try and control the desires of the body by willpower, the Hindu aims at self-realization through the whole being, mind and body.

Certain Hindu and also Buddhist sects worshipped divinities who were particularly concerned with sexual energy, whose teachings were known as "Tantra." This form of sex-worship dates back thousands of years to a mysterious sect of women called *Vratyas*, who acted as sacred harlots or transmitters of divine energy. In due course these practices came to be associated with sacred writings called Tantras, which focused on the divine conjunction of the *lingam*, or penis, and the *yoni*, or vagina, the organs thought to represent cosmic powers. Through their union, the individual could transcend the state of separateness and experience the bliss of union with God. It is clear from the sheer numbers of goddesses in Hindu mythology that female sensuality is an integral part of the Divine. In art, they are represented as reveling in their erotic nature. The idea that the spiritual perfection of womanhood is to be found in the virgin is, in this context, nonsense.

Descriptions of ritual sexual intercourse occur in the Upanishads, which describe the Original Being as being both alone and lonely. He therefore split himself into two parts, which became the original husband and wife and, subsequently, the parents of humanity. A later part of the first Upanishad tells how the Lord of Creatures, Prajapati, created a woman and worshipped her. He then impregnated her. Because she was pregnant the woman was now considered to be sanctified and her vagina, where intercourse took place, became a place of sacrifice. Contact with this place of sacrifice would strengthen a man, and this gave rise to the belief that it was possible, through ritual intercourse, to enjoy the rewards associated with sacrifice, a primitive form of Tantra. However, on a human level, this might not involve quite the degree of worship practiced by Prajapati. In fact, if a man approached a woman who refused him, he was at liberty to use force or bribery.

Tantric rites were practiced by both Buddhists and Hindus. The rites in both cases evolved as a way to achieve release from the conflict and pain of worldly existence by merging into the bliss of nothingness. Enlightenment was sought through a profound sexual experience in which the partners merge to the extent that "each is both," according to the Upanishads. This is in fact an experience which can happen quite spontaneously between two people who are in love and highly attuned to each other. But because it was not expected to be something which occurred as a result of marital sex, in Hinduism at any rate, a married couple would change partners for the practice. Alternatively, a man might call on a specially dedicated temple prostitute. Hindu Tantric rites involved the presence of a guru who would ensure that the rite was properly carried out. Drugs would be involved and a special meal as well.

Closely connected with Hindu Tantric practices was the god Shiva, who takes many forms. The best-known is the Cosmic Dancer, or King of the Dancers, when as god of both creation and destruction he dances form into being and out of it, thus upholding the endless rhythm of life everywhere.

His consort, who is his feminine aspect, or *shakti*, has many names but is often called Parvati. She is the Divine Mother who, like her husband, also has many forms, in her case representing the world of sensation, the feminine energy of the universe. Shiva unites with her as soul to body. In one aspect she is the terrible death goddess Kali, often portrayed wreathed with skulls. There are many myths about this divine pair whose love-play generated so much energy that the other gods were afraid. One story tells how they were visited in their paradise by other gods who found them enjoying sexual intercourse. Ignoring their visitors, they continued their lovemaking. Several of the gods became extremely angry and cursed the pair who, as a result, died still entwined in sexual union. As he died, Shiva declared that his shape from now on would be the *lingam* so that in order to worship him, men must make models of it as objects of veneration. In the same way, Parvati would henceforth be represented by the *yoni*. As a result, as anybody who has visited India will probably know, temples throughout the country, dating from medieval times, are adorned with wonderful sculptures depicting the divine pair in a passionate embrace. These certainly make an interesting contrast with the manner of decoration that ennobles churches in the Western world. The temples at Khajuraho and Konarak are perhaps the best-known in terms of the sexual detail they depict. All manner of positions of sexual intercourse are displayed, while one temple at Konarak shows men with fully erect *lingams* being fellated by female attendants. Such depictions of the sexual act were thought not only to represent eternal orgasmic bliss but also to ward off evil. They may have had the additional benefit of serving as a backlash against forms of Buddhism that banned sexual pleasure. Another theory is that the temples

CENTER: Detail from Lakshmana Temple in Khajuraho, India. These highly erotic temple sculptures show gods and goddesses, representing the masculine and feminine forces of life, in every possible kind of sexual union.

were centers of Tantric practice, possibly inhabited by dedicated harlots for ritual sex.

Despite the teaching in the sixteenth-century sex manual, the *Ananga Ranga*, that sex must be limited to within marriage, most of the classic Indian epics and other texts assume that men would be involved in extramarital sex. Skilled and well-educated courtesans were the Indian equivalent of the geisha in Japan or the *hetaera* in Greece and were held in similar respect. On the other hand, these same texts clearly disapproved of common prostitution. Some high-class prostitutes, however, were attached to Hindu temples, where they served the deities. A little girl would be given to a temple as an offering to the god concerned, usually Krishna or Shiva. She would be known as a *deva-dasi* and considered in many cases to be married to the god. Sometimes the marriage would be marked by a wedding ceremony where the girl would lose her virginity to a priest or perhaps a rich devotee or, on occasion, to a *lingam* made of stone. Subsequently she would learn singing, dancing and the erotic arts. Temple visitors would be able to buy her favors.

So widespread did temple prostitution become that large temples offered hundreds of prostitutes, a source of annoyance and distraction for genuine devotees wishing simply to pray. Towards the end of the nineteenth century, Hindu reformers assisted the British in putting an end to temple prostitution. Many temples have nevertheless preserved the traditional dances, but these are often performed solely by men in an attempt to downplay their erotic qualities.

Exponents of Tantric yoga insisted that Shiva was the supreme god of the Indian pantheon. Seldom depicted alone, his power depended on his union

LEFT and ABOVE: Details from the Lakshmana Temple in Khajuraho, showing the central pillar and the freize.

with his *shakti*. Only as a result of intercourse with her did he have the power to create. Among humans, every orgasm was thought to allow the couple concerned to share in the supreme creative experience of the divinities. When a Tantric yogi united with his partner, or yogini, they therefore represented the union of god and goddess. The yogi could thereby identify himself with Shiva to the extent that at the moment of orgasm he might exclaim, "Shivaham" ("I am Shiva."). As god of sex, Shiva was thought to have advocated that the woman take the superior position in intercourse. Here is a most interesting contrast to the story of Lilith, as we shall see, where the same idea was totally abhorrent to the patriarchy. Shiva is sometimes represented in an androgynous combination with Parvati, to illustrate the unity underlying the apparent duality of the sexes.

Tantra, still widely practiced in India and Nepal, is underpinned by the belief that women have more spiritual energy than men. It follows that a man can experience divinity only through sexual intercourse, usually of a specific kind known as maithuna, involving a form of *coitus reservatus*. The man must ensure that the woman comes to orgasm while he controls himself in order to absorb her sexual energy, considered to have magical properties. In a manner reminiscent of Taoist practice in China, it was considered essential for the man to conserve his vital fluids rather than dissipate them in ejaculation. Doing so would enable him to activate the *kundalini*, the energy situated at the base of the spine, causing it to rise up the spine through the energy centers of the body known as *chakras* and out through the top of the head, so that he achieved enlightenment. Successful practice would free the practitioner from the cycle of life, death, and rebirth. By learning to prolong sexual intercourse, perhaps for hours, he would be like Shiva, the god perpetually in sexual union with his goddess.

Another pair of cosmic lovers in the Hindu pantheon were Krishna and Radha. Like Shiva and Parvati, they served as models of devotion and inspiration through sexual union. Krishna, who appears in the *Bhagavad Gita* as the supreme god, is the subject of other stories which depict him as a cowherd who is irresistible to women. He is a trickster, always up to pranks such as stealing the clothes of the cowgirls when they go bathing so they have to come to him naked in order to get them back. This particular story has been the inspiration for many paintings and was sometimes interpreted as a metaphor for the nakedness of the soul before God. Radha, his consort, was the most beautiful of the cowgirls, and their myth glories in their sexual passion, described in detail, and in which Radha often takes the superior position. Their union is often described as a passionate fight. In the *Gita Govinda*, written in the twelfth century, the development of their relationship includes the all-too-human emotion of jealousy, experienced by Radha as Krishna bestowed his favors on one girl after another. Once the pair were fully united, Krishna had to somehow take care of the remaining cowgirls who wanted him to satisfy them and of whom there were apparently nine hundred thousand – a daunting task. In his devious fashion, he turned himself into that same number of men, the result being surely the greatest instance ever of group intercourse.

Buddhist Tantra is often called *Vajrayana*, meaning "Diamond Vehicle." This tradition claimed that the Buddha had taught that the entire universe is contained within the human body that is powered by the sexual energies. By using these energies in the correct way, liberation could be achieved. Although early Buddhism had given greater significance to the male of the species, the advent of Tantra brought honor to the feminine, and it was even said that, "Buddhahood abides in the Yoni." Divine union was often depicted in sexual imagery in Buddhist art, countless forms of the Buddha being shown in sexual embrace, each with his own *shakti*. In Tibetan Buddhism this divine pair was known as *yab-yam*, meaning the original father and mother. Tibetan Buddhists also revere the goddess Tara, supreme goddess of Mahayana Buddhism. She is the *shakti* of Avalokitesvara, the savior of mankind who leads all sentient beings to enlightenment and as such, she is often depicted sitting on a throne ornamented with lions, symbol of her great power.

A practitioner of Tantric Buddhism believed that he could be raised to a divine level of consciousness through intercourse with a specially initiated woman, known as a *dakini*. These women were reputed to be vessels of divine energy as a result of initiation through sexual union with high Tantric adepts. These were no glamor-girls, and very often were not girls at all, but older women. Such was their supernatural power that they were often pictured in terrifying forms wearing necklaces of human heads dripping blood. Through coitus with a *dakini*, a man would hope to become one with divine power. This was no ordinary sexual encounter but rather a prolonged state of ecstatic meditative intercourse without ejaculation on the man's part. The *dakini's* female energy would interact in a certain way with the masculine, helping to convert the unreleased semen into a magical

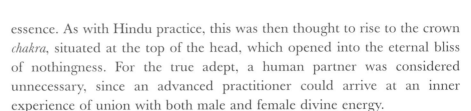

essence. As with Hindu practice, this was then thought to rise to the crown *chakra*, situated at the top of the head, which opened into the eternal bliss of nothingness. For the true adept, a human partner was considered unnecessary, since an advanced practitioner could arrive at an inner experience of union with both male and female divine energy.

The attitude to sexual intercourse in both Tantra and indeed all Oriental sexual practice is fundamentally different from Western attitudes. It focuses on the process and not on the goal of achieving orgasm that is of such concern to Westerners. For Taoists and Tantric practitioners alike, such an attitude is grossly absurd. The pleasure and fulfillment lie, for them, in the exquisite and prolonged experience of ecstasy, affecting both body and soul. Orgasm as a release from built-up tension has no place within this system.

Perhaps the most famous guide to the pleasures of sex ever to have been written is the *Kama Sutra*, probably compiled between the third and fifth centuries AD. Together with its companion text, *Ananga Ranga* and *The Perfumed Garden*, which originated in Arabia, it was first translated into English by Sir Richard Burton just over a hundred years ago. Unlike their modern Western equivalents, the purpose of these manuals was to show people how to unite body and spirit through the sexual encounter. The underlying philosophy was that regular sexual experience of a high quality was essential in order to be a complete human being. Sex, for the early Hindus, was an exciting and spiritually uplifting experience, in no way

Buddhist gods shown in an Indian painting of the mid-19th century.

immoral or forbidden. Apart from sexual positions, the texts give advice on health, sex manners, hygiene, cultivation of the five senses, yoga and successful relationships. They are in fact truly holistic works.

The texts urged experimentation, variety, pleasure, and enjoyment. Contrary to what is often believed, the *Kama Sutra* mentions only three basic positions for sexual intercourse, all the rest are variations on a theme. The names of the positions are descriptive, if perhaps less poetic, than those of the Taoist manuals: the "Yawning Position" where the man is on top with his partner's legs open fairly wide; the "Pair of Tongs" with the woman sitting astride her partner with her knees bent either side

of him; the "Congress of a Cow" in which the man stands behind his partner and enters her from behind while she bends forwards and touches the floor with her hands.

The *Ananga Ranga* dating from around AD 1150, takes the basic positions described in the *Kama Sutra* and explores ways of varying them to prevent sex from becoming monotonous within marriage. Extramarital intercourse being strictly forbidden, the work explains how a husband and wife can live as though they had thirty-two partners. Sexual positions are described as *asanas*, the same word used for the various positions in Hatha Yoga, and are to be carried out slowly and mindfully. Sex, practiced in this way, becomes a form of yoga, a spiritual experience whose aim is to connect with God. It is not just the body which becomes open and receptive but also the soul, with the result that sexual expression becomes far more than a mere fulfillment of bodily needs.

At this time, the Hindu belief system about sexuality was based on the

The Taj Mahal, Agra, India. Perhaps the world's greatest monument to love, it was built by the Shah Jehan as the mausoleum for his favorite and deeply loved wife, who died in childbirth in 1631.

sacred writings contained in the Vedas. Central to this philosophy was the idea of *karma*, a system of cause and effect underpinning an individual's behavior and influencing his or her destiny throughout many incarnations. *Karma* worked on the principle that if you were to cause suffering to another, this was their due for bad behavior in a previous life. You, for your part, as the cause of present suffering, would have to pay the price in some future incarnation. Early Hinduism therefore, unlike Christianity, was not concerned with moral absolutes. The Four Aims, which were the guidelines for good living, were not moral precepts but ways of improving an individual's *karma*. Sex was considered not only a religious duty, as in Chinese Taoism, but also a most enjoyable way of improving one's karma. This attitude had a profound effect on the way relationships were approached and explained some curious ways of behaving recommended in the *Kama Sutra*. For instance, if the girl a man wanted to marry was unwilling, he might try forcing a marriage by first kidnapping and raping her. It could always be argued that the girl had behaved badly in a past life and was now having to settle her karmic debt. On a similar basis, a courtesan who sensed that her lover was losing interest in her was recommended to lose no time in acquiring as many of his valuable possessions as possible.

In spite of recommending what might appear to the Western mind extremely callous forms of behavior, the *Kama Sutra* addressed itself very much to love and was one of the earliest works to connect love and sex. It recommended that men marry for love and acknowledged that a couple who were truly in love would need no manual. Love was sufficient unto itself and such a couple could rely on their instinct and intuition to tell them what to do. Sexual techniques were relevant only to those who were without benefit of what we would call a romantic relationship and therefore stood in need of help. The book therefore made no pretensions to be other than a guide to sexuality, of benefit, for instance, to those who had entered an arranged marriage. The work is full of classifications: four types of love; seven types of intercourse; and different kinds of kisses, embraces, love bites and sounds are all minutely described. Different ways of moving the *lingam*, or penis inside the *yoni*, or vagina are discussed as are, of course, the different sexual positions, the topic most usually associated with the *Kama Sutra*.

The *Kama Sutra* did not limit itself purely to matters sexual. As her principal aim in life the Hindu wife was expected to please her husband,

Detail from the Temple at Lakshmana.

and the book lists the numerous talents, both personal and domestic, which she must acquire to this end. These range from the more traditional occupations of singing, dancing and sewing to swordfighting and the study of magic and sorcery. What it does not offer is advice on contraception since this was considered to interfere with the workings of *karma*. Prostitutes, however, were allowed to practice birth control since it was their *karma* to provide love and pleasure, a process which would be hampered by pregnancy. But they were expected to acquire the relevant knowledge anyway, without recourse to a book.

For the merchant classes who were beginning to grow in importance at this time, the *Kama Sutra* was an especially useful guide. Their new wealth meant that they had more leisure, and they wished to improve their social position. This required the study of correct behavior, particularly in the social sphere. Women, although still subjected to the authority of their menfolk, enjoyed a certain amount of freedom. They were, as ever, thought of as objects of barter but the *Kama Sutra* advised that she who was seen to be most elegantly clad and socially skilled would go to the highest bidder. Young women would therefore go about in society to a degree unthinkable elsewhere. Some were even allowed to choose their own husbands.

Although girls at an earlier epoch of Indian history would usually not marry until they became adults, later religious texts recommended just before puberty as the best age to marry. In the early centuries AD, the ideal age for a bride was considered to be one third that of her groom. By medieval times, it was quite normal for a girl to be married while still a child, although she would not normally go to live with her husband until puberty. This was partly because a girl was considered something of a sexual liability, liable to cause mischief and lose her virginity. The girl would expect to live as part of an extended family since sons would bring their wives to live under the paternal roof, together with their servants.

A girl, being so much younger than her husband, would, more often than not, encounter the horrors of becoming a widow. From medieval times, all women were forbidden to remarry, even child-brides whose marriage had never been consummated owing to the death of the husband. A widow was deprived of all her creature comforts, including her bed, and allowed only one simple meal a day. Perfume and personal ornaments were forbidden. She was required to spend her days in prayer, performing religious rites to ensure that she and her husband would be married again in their next

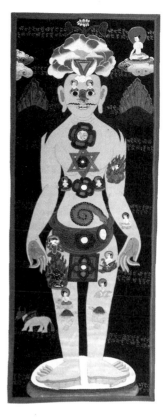

One of a pair of cosmic men in traditional Nepalese or Tibetan style showing the seven chakras and various spiritual points relating to the human constitution.

incarnation. Rather than face such a dreary and joyless existence, many women chose to die with their husbands, a practice known as *suttee*, meaning "a virtuous woman." *Suttee* was not by any means approved of by all authorities, not least because of the possibility of family coercion. It impossible to know how many women elected to join their husbands on the funeral pyre and how many were more or less forced to do so by families for whom they had become superfluous.

OPPOSITE: The exquisitely decorated dome of the "Blue Mosque" of Isfahan, Iran, one of the most famous religious buildings in the world.

Islam: Harem and Mystery

The foundation of the religion of Islam is traditionally marked by the flight of Muhammad from Mecca to Medina in AD 622. It spread rapidly throughout the Near East and into Europe. Islam is akin to the Judeo-Christian tradition in that it is a patriarchal religion venerating a single deity. The word "Islam" means surrender and implies surrendering oneself to the Faith, so that the followers of Muhammad's way became known as Muslims or self-surrenderers. Muhammad is often said to have had nine wives and five concubines, polygamy being the custom in the society of his time. Despite this he apparently lived simply, making frequent retreats into the desert to meditate and pray. On the other hand, certain Muslim writers have emphasized, if not exaggerated, his sexual prowess, ascribing to him the libido of forty men. In fact, the Prophet was twenty-five when he married for the first time. His bride was Khadija, a business-woman of forty, who had been married twice before and was the first to believe his prophetic vocation. Their marriage lasted for twenty-four years and she was the mother of all his children except one. It was only after her death when he was fifty that Muhammad married again, this time a widow. Not until towards the end of his life when he was a prominent religious and political figure did he take other wives, as would have been expected of such a distinguished man. Only one of his wives, the third, had not been married previously. This was Ayesha, who was married to him when she was nine, although she did not live with him until later.

Before the advent of Islam in the seventh century AD, Arabia was a largely matriarchal society. In common with similar cultures, a threefold goddess was worshipped, one of her names being Al-Lat, the original Allah. The first collection of the books of law called the Koran was thought to have been the work of the Seven Sages of earliest times, who were women

Veiled women in a London street, a sight which would have been unthinkable until fairly recent times.

who served as lawgivers. Indeed, the very name of the book means the "Word of Q're." Q're was the Virgin aspect of the triune goddess who shares her name with the Greek Kore, or Persephone. A special goddess, known as Sheba, or the Old Woman, was revered at Mecca as a black stone, marked with the sign of the *yoni*, or vagina. This lay in the sanctuary or *haram*, which was originally a temple of women.

As might be expected, women in pre-Islamic society enjoyed a good deal of independence, free of the veiling and seclusion which was to be the female lot in later times. Because the family system was matriarchal, women were allowed to choose their husbands, and if they were not treated well, to return to their own family. A woman could divorce a husband by the simple expedient of turning her tent to face the east for three consecutive nights. This was a clear message to the man that the marriage was over and further entry to the tent forbidden to him. Polyandry was not uncommon, often involving husbands living in the wife's home, nobody being much concerned which one fathered which child.

A scene from a late-19th century edition of *The Arabian Nights*. The genie commands the young man to slay the princess.

Muhammad changed all this, making monogamy the rule for women so that the identity of a child's father was not in doubt. Divorce now was the prerogative of men who could reject a wife by declaring, "I divorce thee," three times. Nevertheless, in the early period of Islam, women had more independence than was later to be the case and were even allowed to attend prayers in the mosque. The Prophet's wife Ayesha refused to take the veil. Her reasoning was that since God had chosen to make her beautiful, then she should reveal that beauty as a sign of his blessing.

Although there could be no place for a goddess in Islam, she was impossible to eradicate completely. Muhammad was supposed to have had a daughter named Fatima, the name of the earlier Arabian Moon-goddess whose name had many meanings including "Creatress" and "Fate." Fatima was known as the "Mother of her Father," an odd title to give a daughter. Her symbol, the crescent moon, is still found on Islamic flags. Deviant sects within Islam such as the mystical Sufis never ceased to believe that the feminine powers of sexuality and motherhood were what held the universe together. They consequently practiced a form of Tantra. One medieval Sufi poet claimed that true divinity was feminine and that Mecca was in fact the womb of the earth. Not unsurprisingly, those who held such views risked being accused of blasphemy.

In a rather different vein, the Koran has a good deal to say about the relationships between the sexes. The fundamental purpose of marriage was procreation. Girls were to be provided with a dowry and married as soon as they were old enough. On the whole, the Koran seems to favor monogamy simply because it would be difficult to give fair and equable treatment to a number of wives. Although a Muslim man might marry a Jewish or Christian woman if he wished, a Muslim woman could not marry out of her own faith. Both sexes were forbidden to marry a pagan unless they were willing to convert to Islam. Divorce was allowed provided there was an interval of some four months between the separation and the final dissolution of the marriage, so as to make quite sure that the wife was not pregnant. Divorced women would be allowed to keep their dowries. They were allowed to remarry the same husband but not more than three times, unless another marriage had intervened and had ended in divorce.

Sexual intercourse, although it was to be preceded by a prayer, was not considered in any way as a spiritual activity. From the man's point of view, the woman was compared to a furrow to be plowed. Because menstruation

The Turkish Bath, from the painting by Ingres, 1863. A typical 19th century depiction of the harem with the black eunuch in attendance.

was regarded as unclean, however, sexual intercourse was strictly forbidden during that time. There was a great emphasis on cleanliness, and purification by washing was prescribed after a multitude of activities, including sexual activity which did not result in penetration. Nudity under any circumstances was frowned upon. One report said that men should never be naked because recording angels were always present, although they appear to have retired discreetly when a man was excreting or having intercourse. Activities defined as indecent conduct, particularly anal intercourse, or any form of homosexuality, were strictly punished.

Although circumcision was not mentioned in the Koran, it became the traditional practice for both sexes and continues to be so to this day. A boy may be circumcised when seven days old or, as in Egypt, between three and seven, and in some areas up to thirteen. Festivities follow. For a girl, there are no celebrations to accompany the extremely painful operation to which she is subjected. Clitoridectomy was the norm, involving the removal of the tip of the clitoris, but a girl might also undergo total excision of the clitoris and labia minora sometimes accompanied by the sewing up of the vagina.

Apart from the Koran, other writings known as the "Traditions" were greatly revered. These occupied themselves with matters relating to the Prophet and his life so that people might model themselves on him. Muhammad himself respected women and had certainly not chosen to marry submissive females. Unfortunately, patriarchal custom was against him, but the Traditions at least were less strict than the Koran about, for example, touching a woman during menstruation. The Prophet is reported to have condoned all forms of physical affection except intercourse at this time and to have continued to show his wife affection, according to Ayesha. Nevertheless, he is said to have favored marriage with virgins since they would be less demanding. Yet his own marital record appears flatly to contradict his own views. The Prophet's belief in predestination was so strong that he was against any form of contraception, a view not unlike that of some Hindus. Many of the Traditions forbid anal intercourse, which is considered an act of impiety.

Wives were not to be treated unkindly but were expected to be available for sex at any time. Extra-marital activity merited stoning to death although unmarried people who indulged were subject to the lesser punishment of flogging. Although the Prophet based his system of punishments on Jewish law, he apparently recommended adopting a merciful attitude in case the judgment were to prove mistaken. The punishments meted out by strictly orthodox Muslims, such as stoning for adultery and cutting off the hand of a thief, belong to the Traditions and not to the Koran.

During the century following the Prophet's death, Muslims came to dominate vast territories encompassing Syria, Mesopotamia, Persia, North Africa and Spain. Islam therefore absorbed an exceptionally wide and varied body of thought and knowledge with the result that it became, for a time, the repository of almost all known learning. Muhammad himself had laid great stress on learning, and there is no doubt that the intellectual achievements of Islam between the eight and twelfth centuries were quite staggering. From papermaking to mathematics and the invention of stained glass, from metalworking of the most intricate kind to medicine, they

convened and passed on a great body of knowledge, not least to the Christian West. But, as is usually the case when the intellect is given prominence, values relating to the feeling side of life did not develop equally. This inevitably meant that the lot of women did not improve.

Heavenly women, however, were most definitely approved of. According to the Koran, the nature of Paradise is full of sensual delights. The blessed

A view of Constantinople (Istanbul), Turkey from a print dating from 1830.

could look forward to an eternal life spent reclining on couches, enjoying the wine which they were not allowed to drink during their life on earth. For their further gratification they would be ministered to by houris, heavenly women who, although ever-virginal, could provide endless amorous delights to the believer. The female believer could enter heaven as part of a family where she would join her husband to recline on a couch in the shade, eating and drinking whatever she wished.

During the rule of first caliphs, the center of the Islamic empire moved from Medina to Damascus, from where it subsequently shifted to Baghdad. This new city consequently grew to become one of the two principal centers of wealth and culture, equal in stature to Constantinople, at that time the center of Orthodox Christianity. In the eighth century AD, at the height of the flourishing of the city, the fabulous court of the caliph Harun al-Rashid provided the setting for the tales of *The Arabian Nights*. The caliph himself, an educated man, lived in almost outrageous splendor in a palace which occupied about a third of the city. *The Arabian Nights*, sometimes also known as *The Book of a Thousand Nights and One Night*, tells of sexual adventures and orgies and fantastic situations. These are quite definitely stories and romances, in no way meant to constitute a sex manual, of which there was a profusion, particularly in Egypt.

The best-known of the Islamic sex manuals is undoubtedly *The Perfumed Garden for the Soul's Delectation*, written in the sixteenth century. It focuses on the enjoyment of sexual pleasure but not on any mystical experience to be gained through it. A whole range of subjects is discussed including different sexual positions, with eleven main ones noted. Lists of different names for the sexual organs are given, together with information about sterility, abortion, impotence, aphrodisiacs, and other topics. Stories are told, largely to demonstrate the deceitfulness of the female of the species. The author was aware of the existence of the Indian sex manuals and described another twenty-five positions for intercourse. He noted that these were said to be practiced by the Indians, who were more advanced in their knowledge of coitus.

It was after the move of the court to Baghdad that the veiling of women seems to have become compulsory. The Prophet had eventually introduced a degree of veiling into his own household. His wives were expected to be different from ordinary women and to behave with greater modesty and dignity. This involved covering themselves to some extent with a mantle although he does not seem to have required them to veil their faces. Visitors were only allowed to speak to the wives from behind a curtain. It is perhaps here that we have the first intimations of the harem, together with the Prophet's insistence that a man could take more than one wife only if he felt able to treat them all with an equal degree of kindness. It therefore became the custom to give each wife her own separate quarters, which could range from a room to a house, if the man were rich enough. But this brought with it the dangers of a wife finding it relatively easy to indulge in extramarital liaisons. Since Arabs were convinced of the treachery of women, the answer, they felt, was to lock them up in their quarters.

For the origin of the word "harem" we have to look back to the great goddess Ishtar who, in her role as patroness of temple prostitutes or *harines*, was known as Har. The part of the temple occupied by the priestesses came to be called the Harem or Sanctuary. Both harlot and *houri* come from the same root. Some authorities give an alternative meaning for the word, namely "forbidden," indicating that the female inhabitants of the harem were strictly out of bounds to men

A version of the Koran from AD 704.

other than their husband. The heyday of the harem, so to speak, came after 1453 when the Ottoman Turks finally overthrew the remains of the Byzantine Empire. As is the case with so many conquerors, they adopted many of the customs of their Arab predecessors and took wholeheartedly to the notion of the harem.

For hundreds of years, nothing was revealed to the outside world about the harem of the ruler. In consequence it became a source of myth, mystery and fantasy which fed the Western imagination for generations. We know now that the sultan's harem was vast, with up to twelve hundred concubines in residence and almost never less than three hundred. Of these, the majority would have been purchased in the slave markets of the Mediterranean and the Black Sea while others were simply captured and presented as gifts to the sultan. The popular picture of the harem is of voluptuous women lounging around on sofas eating sweetmeats while awaiting the call to the caliph's bed. But the more prosaic reality was that the girls were taught skills and given jobs to do as embroiderers, musicians, and even bookkeepers. Some concubines were destined never to set foot in the sultan's bedroom and were in due course pensioned off and sent to live in retirement with others in the same situation. When a girl did attract the attention of the sultan, she would be elaborately prepared for her encounter with him before being taken to his bedchamber. Protocol for joining him required her to climb into the foot of the bed, under the coverlet, and make her way up until she was finally level with him.

If she were so fortunate as to bear a son, the concubine would be given the privileged rank of *kadin*. Now came her opportunity to exercise her political skills in order to improve her own standing and that of her child. When a sultan died, the sons could, and often did, fight ferociously for the succession. Indeed, up until the seventeenth century, the Law of Fratricide required that the son who succeeded his father must kill all his brothers. Doubtless he would already have done so anyway in order to attain this position. Because the power in the harem belonged to the mother of the sultan, known as the Sultan Valideh, this was the position the more senior of the *kadins* aspired to. A woman in this position must be fiercely ambitious, a mistress of intrigue. She must do all she could in order to draw her son to the sultan's attention and ensure he was looked upon favorably. A truly clever *kadin* would also know how to subject her son to her influence. If he subsequently became sultan, she could then look forward to wielding power far beyond the confines of the harem. One of the most successful of all the *kadins* was the Russian, Roxelana Sultan. Her talents were such that she became the wife of Suleiman the Magnificent and exercised considerable influence over the political manoeuvres of the time.

Within the harem, the concubines were guarded by eunuchs, whose numbers could run into hundreds. Nobody knows with certainty where the concept of a eunuch first originated but there were Assyrian laws dating back hundreds of years BC which allowed a man who caught his wife *in flagrante* to castrate the offending male. When the Persians took over the

Dancing girls in an Egyptian harem from an engraving dated 1804.

Assyrian empire, they were known to have practiced the castration of prisoners, who might well be employed as eunuchs. During the period of the Byzantine empire, several posts in high office were reserved for eunuchs, presumably because they could be relied upon to be loyal, having no family interests to consider. The result of this policy was that parents with several sons would have one castrated in order to further his career and, in consequence, that of his brothers.

Although other male servants at court were forbidden to enter the harem, as indeed were males in general, eunuchs, having been rendered harmless, spent their whole time there. If the stories in the *Thousand and One Nights* are to be believed, however, some eunuchs were quite capable of sexual intimacy. Presumably they had been subjected to the removal of their testicles only, which tended to be the case with white eunuchs. The less fortunate black slaves from Africa usually had all their external organs removed before they were assigned to harem duty. However, the chief black eunuch occupied a position of immense privilege and was the only person allowed to meet with the sultan at any time.

CHAPTER 5

Religion and Taboo

Judaism

IN THE WESTERN WORLD, it was the ancient Hebrews who most profoundly influenced the development of attitudes to sexuality. They were the founders of Judaism between 4000–2000 BC, a highly patriarchal religion, which subsequently gave birth to both Christianity and Islam. In fact, a viable Jewish state of Israel existed for a relatively brief period of time after the return from exile in Egypt in 538 BC. It is therefore a tribute to the genius of this people that they preserved their identity throughout periods of exile, repression and occupation. What enabled them to do this was a system of religious laws based on the teachings of Moses, around 540 BC. Because these laws were held to be commandments from God, an individual who transgressed would automatically be responsible for causing divine wrath to fall upon the community. Obedience to the law, therefore, was paramount.

The laws concerning sexual behavior were no exception. God had commanded the Jews to "...be fruitful and multiply." Sexual activity was

OPPOSITE: *The Fall,* from the painting by Hugo van der Goes, c.1440-82. The serpent is shown as another form of Eve, the feminine principle. In the esoteric tradition, the serpent was often seen as a symbol of wisdom but for the Christians it signified evil.

therefore first and foremost for the purpose of procreation and was allowable only within the context of marriage, which was considered a religious obligation. It was impossible for an unmarried man to become a priest because it was believed that his prayers and invocations would have no power. According to the scriptures, the Hebrew view was, that "...the man who has neither wife nor children is disgraced in the world and is hated by them, like a leafless and fruitless tree." Homosexuality, according to the book of Leviticus, merited the death penalty, while transvestism was considered insulting to God.

Early marriage was encouraged in order to protect the morals of the people. A boy could expect to be about fifteen when he married, a girl somewhat younger. So seriously was marriage taken that if a boy had not found a wife by the time he was eighteen, he might have to explain himself to the elders of the community. Within this society there was no place for a single person: even widows and widowers were obliged to remarry as soon as possible. All children, even those born out of wedlock, were considered legitimate unless they were the result of forbidden unions such as incest or adultery. Incest was absolutely taboo and always punished.

Little is known about the techniques of sex practiced by the early Hebrews, although within marriage there appears to have been considerable freedom of sexual expression. It was clearly acknowledged that sex, although a marital duty, was in itself inherently pleasurable and to be indulged in freely. Indeed, those of private means who therefore presumably did little work, were required to make love every day. Even a lowly camel driver must make sure he had intercourse with his wife at least once a month. Sexual relations were allowed during pregnancy and nursing and even if a woman was unable to bear a child or was post-menopausal, her husband must continue to satisfy her. The issue here was not the woman's feelings but rather the need to allow for miracles of conception if God so wished, as in the case of Sarah, the wife of Abraham who bore his son Isaac when Abraham was a hundred years old.

In the earliest period of Judaism, before about 600 BC, the code of sexual behavior was relatively simple. However, after they had been driven out of Israel by the Canaanites, and during the period of exile in Egypt which ended in 538 BC, attitudes changed quite considerably. Once Jews no longer had a homeland of their own, the community had to be protected from assimilation into other cultures. To this end, rules came into being which clarified exactly how a Jew must behave in order to distinguish him or herself from a non-Jew. This naturally served to make intermarriage extremely difficult. The rules emphasized man's weaknesses, of which the greatest was considered to be his sexual desires. A rigid code of morality developed, and even the more liberally-inclined were subject to strict rules concerning sex. These dour attitudes were later to become incorporated into Christianity and were a key factor in the Christian attitude of hostility towards expressions of sexuality.

For the key to the relative position of the two sexes, we have to look back to the story of Adam and Eve. We are told that the serpent seduced Eve into handing Adam the apple and thus caused him to disobey God. Eve is subsequently identified with the serpent, sin, and seduction. For this she had to be punished. From then on, within the collective psyche of the Judeo-Christian tradition, woman were considered inferior. We live with the fallout of this view to this day. In most cultures, however, the serpent

Samson and Delilah, from the painting by Felice Gianni, 1760-1823.
Samson was betrayed by Delilah who cut off his hair the source of his strength.

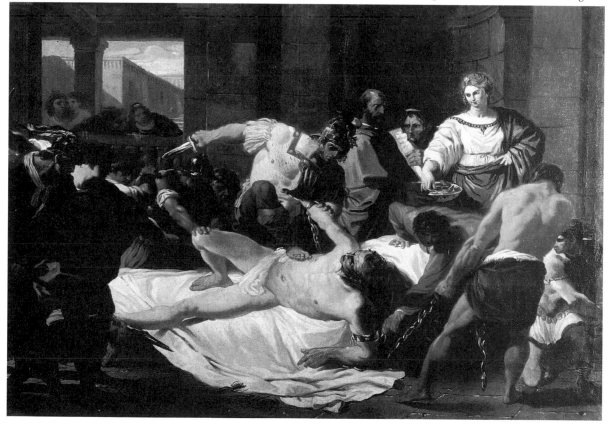

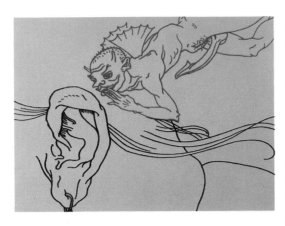

An incubus whispering lustful thoughts into the ear of a woman. From a Russian drawing.

OPPOSITE: *Susanna and the Elders,* from the painting by Rembrandt, 1606-69. Susanna, condemned to die on a false charge of adultery brought by two elders whose advances she had spurned, was saved by the prophet Daniel.

stands for something very positive, quite often wisdom or rebirth, because it sheds its skin. Serpents were also associated with worship of the Goddess. The early Hebrews, as we shall see, set out to stamp out goddess worship, which is probably why the serpent is shown in such an unfavorable light in the Book of Genesis. A very old Sumerian seal, dating back to around 3500 BC, depicts the goddess, the serpent, and the tree from which the goddess is handing the fruit of life to a man. Other seals show her with a plant emerging from her genitals. With the advent of worship of Jehovah, the god of the Old Testament, man became supreme and the idea of a goddess as life-giver became anathema.

The supremacy accorded to the male relegated the woman's role to that of serving the man, particularly in view of the fact that Eve had led Adam astray. To this day, an Orthodox man recites a daily prayer thanking God for not making him a woman. Women, considered to be essentially seductive, were thought therefore to have an insatiable desire for sex. Several of the stories in the Old Testament illustrate the Judaistic belief that women would not hesitate to use their sexuality in order to outwit defenseless men. Among these seductresses are Delilah, who deprived Samson of his strength and whose name, interestingly, means "she who makes weak"; and Potiphar's wife, who attempted to seduce, and then destroy, Joseph.

A powerful woman like Deborah is referred to as a "prophetess," which was, apparently, an acceptable status for a woman. In general, however, the Jewish patriarchs seem to have felt extremely threatened by a woman's power and in particular by her ability to cast spells. This she would apparently do by pointing the index finger in an aggressive way, for which reason women were required to wear their wedding rings on this finger as a way of fettering it. Christians did not take up this tradition but instead copied the pagan custom of wearing the ring on the fourth finger of the left hand, from where a mystical love vein was thought to run directly to the heart.

Women were thought to be so obsessed with sex that they might resort to bestiality to satisfy their lust. The Talmud, the body of legend, law and rabbinic commentaries on the Old Testament scriptures, forbids this

practice to the extent that a widow is not allowed to keep a pet dog. Nor may she keep a slave, presumably on account of the danger of her being overcome by her voracious desires. Within marriage, however, a woman's need for sexual pleasure was recognized in a more positive way: the Talmud makes it clear that it is a husband's duty to satisfy his wife. His sexual prowess brought other advantages, since it was believed that by bringing his wife to orgasm before himself, a man could ensure the conception of a son. So seriously were a man's sexual duties taken that it was forbidden, by one authority at any rate, for him to take more than four wives. This was deemed to be the maximum number for which he would be able to find the energy necessary to give equal attention to each. A multiplicity of wives is not uncommon in the Old Testament itself, perhaps the most famous example being King Solomon, who apparently had seven hundred wives.

Prejudice against the feminine is also revealed in the definition of adultery. This was deemed a capital offense but applied only to the sexual congress of a married woman with a man other than her husband. A man who enjoyed an extramarital liaison was not considered adulterous. The matter of rape is also dealt with in a curious way, particularly in the Talmud. The official view was that it would be almost impossible for a woman to be raped since, although she may at first resent this attack upon her person, her insatiable lust would most likely turn her resistance into subsequent consent. During warfare it was the standard practice for Hebrew soldiers to rape captured women.

One Biblical woman who refused to allow herself to be raped was Judith, whose story appears in the Apocrypha. The Jews were on the point of surrender to Holofernes, the Assyrian general who had been sent to punish them for refusing to help the Assyrians in their war against the Medes. Judith, a young and devout Jewish widow, took her countrymen to task for their lack of faith and decided to take matters into her own hands. Entering the enemy camp, she pretended to be a prophetess, come to pray that the sins of her people might be uncovered. She explained that God, to demonstrate his anger with the Jews for disobeying his rules, would ensure an Assyrian victory. On the fourth day of her visit Holofernes, much smitten with her beauty, invited Judith to dine with him. During the meal he drank far too much and fell into an unconscious stupor before he was able to make any advances to her. Judith proceeded to take his sword and use it to cut off his head. This she placed in a sack and took back home, where it was displayed high on the city walls, causing mayhem among the waiting Assyrian troops who fled in panic and were slaughtered. By her unswerving faith and courage, along with a large measure of cunning and deceit, Judith had saved her people.

Another Apocryphal text about the strength of a woman's faith against all the odds is that of Susanna, a respectable young Jewish wife. A pair of lecherous elders hid themselves in order to spy on her as she washed. Revealing themselves, they threatened to accuse her of adultery with a young man unless she consented to have sex with them. Susanna refused, preferring to risk the consequences of slander, despite the consequent possibility of suffering death by stoning. In the recounted event, she was brought to trial and condemned. However, divine intervention saved her in the person of a young man called Daniel, who proved that the two men were lying. This is a particularly interesting counterpart to the standard view of women as creatures so lustful that they even welcomed rape.

As a patriarchal religion, Judaism regarded the phallus with great reverence. Even a castrated animal was not an acceptable offering on an altar. Great attention was paid to the protection of the penis and women were forbidden to injure a man's testicles in any way. In the Book of Deuteronomy we read that a woman who grasps a man's private parts is to have her hand cut off, even if her act was meant to protect him against an enemy. In previous times, a sacred king, upon accession to the throne, had to eat the genitals of the one he had deposed in order to absorb the holy power they were thought to contain as a result of intimate union with the goddess-queen. That this practice was outlawed by the Hebrews is made clear at the end of the story of Jacob wrestling with God. "Therefore the children of Israel eat not of the sinew which shrank, which is upon the hollow of the thigh to this day..." (Gen. 32:32). It is interesting to note the words used to describe the penis, a word avoided by the prophets and rabbis in case evil spirits were drawn to it.

Allied with the devotion to the male member was the rite

Phoenician stele, or carved pillar, which shows the Canaanite fertility god, Baal, c.1900 BC.

The Tree of Life, from a clay tablet of Assurbanipal, the last King of Assyria.

of circumcision. According to the Bible, this ritual was introduced as a result of the covenant made by Abraham with God and was a requirement for every newborn boy as a sign of acceptance into the Jewish faith. To be uncircumcised would be to break the covenant and invite being cast out from the Jewish people. Flint knives, mentioned in the stories of Joshua and of Moses, were ceremonially required in order to perform the operation, which we may therefore assume was a very ancient tradition. Originally carried out by the boy's father, the rite was later conducted by a special surgeon and followed by a party.

In the Talmud, masturbation was strongly forbidden. One writer even regarded it as a crime deserving the death penalty. "And if a man's seed of copulation go out from him, then he shall wash all his flesh in water, and be unclean until the evening. And every garment, and every skin, whereupon is the seed of copulation, shall be washed with water, and be unclean until the evening." Why was this? Perhaps it implied the failure of the male's duty to procreate and replenish the earth. This makes sense when we understand that the ancient Hebrews regarded the male semen as the key to conception. It could therefore be deposited only in a woman's vagina and nowhere else. The role of woman was simply that of a receptacle in which the seed could grow and develop.

In contrast with the respect accorded to the phallus, any indications of sexuality in a woman were severely repressed. Menstruation was regarded with a degree of horror, which is curious in view of the fact that it was presumably part of God's creation. During her period a woman was considered unclean, as was anything or anybody she touched during this time. If a couple were found to have had sexual intercourse during menstruation they risked being expelled from the community. In later Judaism the period of uncleanliness was terminated by the rite of the *mikvah* or traditional bath still required of Orthodox Jewish women. After childbirth a woman was also considered unclean and had to undergo a thirty-three-day period of purification.

Hair was thought of as another dangerous area. An ancient belief held that women needed their hair in order to work magic spells. By definition, therefore, those who were deprived of their hair were rendered harmless. For this reason, Jewish wives were compelled to shave their heads, a rule later applied to Christian nuns. Even today an Orthodox Jewish wife continues the tradition by wearing a wig.

Divorce was a simple matter for a man, at any rate. In a patriarchal system, the husband had the authority and could divorce his wife even against her wishes. He, on the other hand, could only be divorced with his full agreement. The eleventh-century reform of the divorce law stipulated that a wife had to consent for a divorce to be granted. One serious drawback to divorce as far as the man was concerned was that he must

An incubus sitting on the breast of a sleeping woman. According to one legend, an incubus was a fallen angel who had succumbed to the sin of lust. From an engraving based on the painting *The Nightmare,* by Henry Fuseli, c.1840.

repay to his wife the sum of their marriage settlement. However, if her conduct was bad enough to create scandal, an exception would be made. Perhaps it need not surprise us that "scandal" might be defined as going out with her head uncovered or being noisy in a public place.

Within the context of such a strictly patriarchal religion, it is extraordinary that the Old Testament scriptures contain, in complete contrast, "The Song of Solomon." This collection of love poems of a deeply sensual and joyful nature may, as some scholars have contested, be a metaphor for the relationship between God and Israel. Be that as it may, these rhapsodic verses celebrate sexual love in a way reminiscent of the Song of Inanna. "Let him kiss me with the kisses of his mouth: for thy love is better than wine," says the woman while he declares: "Thy navel is like a round goblet, which wanteth not liquor: thy belly is like an heap of wheat set about with lilies. Thy two breasts are like two young roes that are twins."

The Jewish Cabbalists of medieval times used sexual language to describe the relationship between God and the *Shekhinah*, his female soul, or indwelling spirit. Their representation of the Tree of Life showed the *Shekhinah* at the very top of the tree, manifesting the presence of God in the universe. The Cabbalists believed that evil was the result of God's loss of his *Shekhinah*. To reunite the male and female principles, therefore, sex magic was essential, a principle which harks back to the sacred marriage of earlier times. Couples were encouraged to engage in intercourse on the Sabbath so that the other six days of the week might be blessed. The Sabbath is personified as a goddess known as the Sabbath Bride, who is welcomed with the lighting of candles and singing of special prayers on Friday night. To this day, it is the woman of the house who lights the candles and recites the special prayer.

In the writings of the orthodox Hasidic sect, erotic terminology is used in abundance. The swaying which characterizes Hasidic prayer, such as one sees to this day at the Wailing Wall in Jerusalem, is compared to the movements made at the beginning of sexual intercourse. By moving in a similar way, a man could have intercourse with the *Shekhinah*, a state of mystical ecstasy.

Underpinning the anti-feminine bias of Judaism was the enormous difficulty of eradicating the goddess-worship prevalent in Canaan and adopted by the Hebrew tribes who settled there. As is often the case with settlers, they took over the mythology, cult sites, feasts, and rites of the indigenous people. Despite the best efforts of the prophets, it proved extremely difficult to replace the old beliefs, which involved temple priestesses and sexual fertility rites, with Jehovah, the voice of the Law. For the Hebrews, whose language contained no word meaning "goddess," there could obviously be no priestesses. The orders given in Leviticus 19:29, "Do not prostitute thy daughter to cause her to be a whore; lest the land fall to whoredom, and the land become full of wickedness," were given to ensure that the Hebrews did not follow the Babylonian custom whereby a girl offered her virginity to the goddess before marriage, or allow their daughters to become temple prostitutes. Yet old customs die hard, and it was only with considerable tenacity that the rabbis managed to stamp out goddess worship. Even then, the image of the goddess survived for a long time. Many of the Old Testament stories need to be read with this in mind.

The Babylonian figure of Lilith, sometimes known as the Lady of the Beasts.

Among the principal Canaanite goddesses were Asherah, Astarte, and Anath, all of whom had much in common with contemporary goddesses in Babylon and Egypt. Anath's brother-consort, Baal, often depicted as a bull, is referred to often in the Old Testament. The bull, of course, is often credited with tremendous sexual power. When Aaron told the Israelites to make a golden calf and worship it, he was in fact encouraging them to enact the rites associated both with Anath and also with the Egyptian goddess Hathor, who was said to have daily given birth to the sun, Horus-Ra, who was her Golden Calf. This would account for the fact that the participants in the ceremonies were naked and apparently holding an orgiastic feast when they were discovered by Moses. Astarte was worshipped at the court of King Ahab, who ruled Israel from 873–852 BC, and his queen, Jezebel, a princess of Sidon who would therefore have been quite accustomed to the worship of the goddess. The royal pair were murdered during a civil war begun by the supporters of Jehovah.

The prophet Jeremiah had particular trouble with the old beliefs. Speaking to those Jews who were in exile in Egypt, he blamed the catastrophe of the Exile on their worship of Ishtar, the Queen of Heaven. Those he addressed, however, took the opposite view, insisting that trouble had befallen them as a result of their neglect of the goddess, who had therefore deserted them. Jeremiah's view was that God was the divine bridegroom of the Israelites who had therefore, by worshipping the goddess, "played the harlot with many lovers." The papyri discovered at Elephantine, in Upper Egypt, show that a Jewish military colony there had worshipped both Jehovah and a god called Anathyahu, thought to be Anath as the spouse of Jehovah

Further echoes of goddess-worship are found in the story of Lilith who was, according to legend, Adam's first wife. Perhaps she solves the puzzle of the two creation myths in the Book of Genesis where we learn first that, "So God created man in his own image, in the image of God created he him; male and female created he them" (Gen. 1:27). In contrast, we subsequently learn that, "The Lord God caused a deep sleep to fall upon Adam, and he slept: and he took one of his ribs, and closed up the flesh instead thereof; And the rib, which the Lord God had taken from man, made he a woman, and brought her unto the man." (Gen. 2:21-22).

An ancient Jewish text gives us this account of her origins:

> "God formed Lilith the first woman just as He had formed Adam except that he used filth and impure sediment instead of dust or earth. Adam and Lilith never found peace together. She disagreed with him in many matters... and refused to lie beneath him in sexual intercourse, basing her claim of equality on the fact that each had been created from earth. When Lilith saw that Adam would overpower her, she uttered the ineffable name of God and flew up into the air of the world. Eventually, she dwelt in a cave in the desert on the shores of the Red Sea. There she engaged in unbridled promiscuity, consorted with lascivious demons, and gave birth to hundreds of Lilim, or demonic babies, daily."

Lilith's refusal to confine herself to assuming the inferior position was to have major repercussions. From her desert abode, it was said that she continually acted out her jealousy and anger towards Eve and all of Eve's children. She had a reputation not only for killing children but for

preventing birth by inflicting infertility, causing miscarriages and producing fatal complications during childbirth. So much was her influence feared that in many Jewish homes from the seventh century AD onwards were to be found amulets or bowls inscribed with her name or the names of angels who could protect the inhabitants against her evil influence. Her daughters were lustful she-demons who would copulate with men in their dreams, squatting on top of their victims and causing nocturnal emissions. As late as the Middle Ages Jews were still manufacturing amulets to protect them from the *lilim*, who were eventually to be adopted by Christians, who called

Adam and Eve, from the painting by William Strang, 1859-1929. A Victorian rendering of a reluctant Adam being pressed by Eve to eat the apple.
"The woman whom thou gavest to be with me, she gave me of the tree, and I did eat." Gen. 1:12

them succubae. To keep them at bay, celibate monks would sleep with their hands crossed over their genitals, clutching a crucifix and hoping for a good night's sleep.

In *The Panarion*, written in the fourth century AD, Epiphanius relates the views of a Gnostic sect concerning Lilith and Elijah, which he evidently found somewhat alarming:

> *"So that they also dare to blaspheme concerning Saint Elijah and dare to maintain that he (Philippus) says that when he (Elijah) was carried up to Heaven, he was thrown back again into the cosmos. For there came, so they say, a female demon who proved herself the stronger and asked him whither he was going.*
> *'For I have children by you,' she said, 'and (therefore) thou canst not rise up and leave thy children in the lurch.'*
> *And he (Elijah) said (Philippus relates),*
> *'How canst thou have children by me, for I lived chastely?'*
> *But she said to him, so they tell,*
> *'Nevertheless when thou didst dream in thy sleep, thou didst often relieve thyself by an emission of semen. It was I that took the sperm from thee and bare thee sons.'"*
> (The Panarion 26:13, 4-5).

Later, Lilith was to appear in the *Zohar*, the Cabbalistic work of the thirteenth century which is, essentially, a meditation on the Old Testament. Here, oddly enough, she tended to receive a quite different press. A Spanish Cabbalist of the twelfth century, R. Isaac Hacohen, wrote that, "Lilith is a ladder on which one can ascend to the rungs of prophecy." While in the sixteenth century, a Cabbalist named Hayyim Vital declared that it is Lilith who is, by night, at any rate, the angel called the "flame of the revolving sword." In other writings, she appears in the guise of the nakedness of the *Shekhinah* or Holy Spirit, during the time of Israel's exile. According to a sixteenth-century Cabbalistic story, God cast off his consort, known as the *Matronit*, after the destruction of the Temple, and took Lilith to be his bride in her place.

It is perhaps in this legend that we see the beginning of the ambivalent attitude towards women which has characterized Judeo-Christian culture ever since. Lilith represents the dark, instinctual, untameable aspect of the feminine nature who demands from a man both equality and respect. Eve, on the other hand, is altogether more obedient, domesticated and gentle, the perfect wife and mother whose qualities were later celebrated in the

Virgin Mary. These myths were to have enormous repercussions within Western society and indeed continue to do so to this day.

Christianity Usurps the Pagan Festivals

Christianity is made up of a complex assortment of myths and belief systems. What began as the beliefs of a small Jewish sect developed into an international religion, influenced not only by its Hebrew origins, but also by the cultures with which it came into contact, notably Greece and Rome. Christianity spread to Rome soon after the death of Christ but it was not until the time of the Emperor Constantine I, c.AD 274-337 , that it became the official religion of Rome. The Edict of Milan, AD 313, gave civil rights and toleration to Christians and Christianity became the state religion in 324, although Constantine himself, who murdered many of his close relatives, was hardly a model Christian and in fact considered himself to be the incarnation of a god. The popularity of the new religion was partly a reaction against the state of extreme corruption and decadence which now characterized the once-great Roman Empire.

A young wife hands her lover the key to her chastity belt with one hand, whilst with the other she steals her husband's money as he fondles her. From a late 15th century woodcut by Hans Baldung

The story of Jesus has strong mythical overtones of other saviors who were born of a virgin, suffered. died, descended to the underworld, and were reborn. Early Christian believers required their own Savior to have similar attributes and he was therefore credited with a virgin mother. In this way, Mary was continuing in the tradition of goddesses such as Ishtar and Isis, beloved of ancient peoples. The harlot-priestesses of Ishtar, like those of Greek Aphrodite and Asherah of Canaan, were often referred to as "Holy Virgins." The word "virgin" in this context translates as "unmarried" and has nothing to do with a physical state of virginity, which was obviously inapplicable to these priestesses. "Holy virgins," as we have seen, channelled the energy of the goddess through ritual sexual worship, and their children were referred to as "virgin-born." One school of belief holds that Mary herself was such a priestess and points to the Gospel of Luke where we are told that the angel Gabriel "came in unto her," a phrase which in biblical terms means having sexual intercourse. The name Gabriel means, literally, "divine husband."

Another, second-century source, the *Protoevangelium of James*, tells how Joachim and Anna, Mary's parents, begged God to grant them a child. Anna was then visited by an angel who told her that God had heard her prayers and that she could expect to conceive and bear a child. As a mark of gratitude, Anna vowed that she would offer the child to God's temple. When Mary was three years old, her mother carried out her promise and the girl lived a life apart in the temple until she was thirteen. At that point Joseph, her future husband, was found for her by sacred lot. Although this story also makes Mary a temple virgin, the temple in question was obviously not dedicated to the goddess.

The Church fathers were well aware of the affection in which Mary was held and went to great lengths to ensure that there would be no resurgence of goddess worship. But the need for a feminine deity persisted. Mary has been depicted throughout the centuries as the Great Mother, protecting human beings from harm by gathering them in her robe and as Queen of Heaven, like Ishtar and Inanna before her. Like them, she is sometimes depicted standing upon a crescent moon. Medieval illustrations show her as an Earth goddess, surrounded by corn, in the manner of the Greek Demeter. Her mourning for her son echoes the lament of Isis for Osiris, Cybele for Attis, and numerous other goddesses whose son-lovers died and usually were subsequently reborn.

Although Jesus and his disciples were all Jewish, they departed radically from the sexual traditions of Judaism. Jesus himself was celibate which, for a rabbi, would have been unthinkable. To the Jewish mind, the celibate state was both unnatural and immoral. In an effort to understand this anomaly, writers in recent years have suggested that Jesus was in fact married to Mary Magdalene, or perhaps that he belonged to the ascetic Essene sect, or, alternatively, that he was homosexual. Whatever the case, what we do know is that in sexual matters, as in other areas, he emphasized forgiveness rather than sin. Although Jesus came down firmly in favor of monogamy – and Christianity was the first major religion which, from its very beginnings insisted on monogamy – he prescribed leniency in the case of the woman taken in adultery, and refused to condemn her. Although he is assumed to have taken a hard line on divorce, decreeing that, "What God

Scenes from the Life of Jesus. Mother and Child.
From the frescoes by Fra Angelico, San Marco, Florence.
Mary, whose virginity was considered to have redeemed the sin of Eve, was proposed by the Church as a role-model for women, an impossible position to maintain.

has joined together, let not man put asunder," this was at least in part to counteract the ease with which a Jewish man might divorce his wife.

St. Paul, however, went much further in his pursuit of sexual sin. In fact, he thought celibacy the preferred state, since it would allow the believer more time to devote to the Lord. For those not called to the celibate life, however, he felt that marriage was essential – "It is better to marry than to burn" (presumably with desire) – but he considered that marriage must be a spiritual as well as physical union. His thinking here was not traditionally Hebraic but more akin to that of certain Gnostic beliefs. Much more traditionally Jewish was his view that married couples must not deny sexual relations to each other. "The wife hath not power of her own body, but the husband; and likewise also the husband hath not power of his own body, but the wife." (I Cor. 7:4).

There is no denying that St. Paul had no very great opinion of women. In his view, woman had been created for the benefit of man and must therefore defer to him in everything, obedience being the price she must pay for Eve's sin in leading Adam astray. The early Church Fathers, whose views were to have a definitive influence on sexual attitudes, were no more enthusiastic about the feminine. Particularly influential was St. Augustine, whose personal struggle with his own sexual nature is recorded in his *Confessions*, where perhaps his most famous words are recorded, "Give me chastity – but not yet." For the first thirty years of his life he had led a dissolute existence, which came to an end when he converted to Christianity, at which point he renounced sexual activity altogether.

Augustine quickly became an influential member of the Roman Catholic Church and in due course was made a bishop. His writings clearly indicate that he associated sexuality with guilt, which lead him to insist that celibacy was a higher moral state than marriage. Even marital sexual intercourse was, in his view, sinful, since the emotions accompanying it were shameful. It was of course necessary to have children, but infant baptism was essential in order to wash away the guilt of lust. It is interesting to note that Augustine was writing in the fifth century AD, not so very long after the times when the act of sex had been celebrated in the temples as a religious observance.

One aspect of goddess worship which lasted for a very long time was its effect upon the ritual of marriage. The root of the word, the Latin *maritare*, implied union under the auspices of the goddess Aphrodite-Mari, whose help was invoked in all aspects of marriage. The idea of a male priest presiding over a marriage ceremony was therefore so unthinkable that for many centuries marriage remained under the auspices of common law. Mere cohabitation could constitute a valid marriage, especially among the peasant classes where land and dowries were not an issue. In very early Christian times the marriage ceremony consisted of a blessing of the couple outside the closed doors of the church, so that lustful vibrations might not contaminate the house of the Lord.

Until the sixteenth century there was no Christian sacrament of marriage. Among the Celts there had been a system of group marriage, an ancient tradition dating back to the Great Goddess Rhea, who declared monogamy to be a sin. It was not until 1753 that the blessing of the Church became a legal requirement for marriage in England. In Scotland, however, it continued to be possible to be legally married by the old pagan custom whereby the couple's hands were joined in the presence of witnesses with

Festival of Britons, Stonehenge. A Victorian representation of a Druid religious celebration at this mysterious stone circle whose precise purpose remains unknown. It possibly served as an observatory.

no requirement for a clergyman. As a result, there grew up a tradition of elopement over the Border to Gretna Green. Once the pagan marriage laws had been revised, any property owned by the wife was placed under her husband's control. This emphasis on total ownership of the woman was epitomized in the chastity belt of medieval times. Constructed upon a metal framework, it had two holes which were just large enough to allow normal bodily functions but made penetration an impossibility. A jealous husband could lock the belt over his wife's hips and keep the key, confident that she would live a nun-like existence while he was away from home.

As Christianity spread into Europe, it had to contend with paganism, the practice of worship of the old gods and goddesses which country folk in particular clung to. Shrewdly, the Church allowed paganism to continue while gradually taking over the holy places, customs, and holidays, making them its own. The virgin mother and child, death and resurrection, salvation of the soul, and other doctrines which purport to be intrinsically Christian, had in fact developed centuries before .

Most of the pagan festivals later subsumed into Christianity were connected with fertility and had originally involved sexual rites of some kind. Easter, for instance, was originally a springtime festival of sacrifice in honor of the Saxon goddess Eostre, whose name gives us the word for the female hormone, oestrogen. The date used to fix Easter Sunday, namely the first Sunday following the first full moon after the spring equinox, was originally the time when Eostre was thought to have become pregnant and the earth was passing into the fertile season.

Christmas itself was not officially celebrated until late in the fourth century and what we think of as traditional festivities are almost entirely pagan in origin. The date chosen, 25 December, coincided with the festival of the birth of the new light, or Divine Child, at the time of what used to be the winter solstice. The Persian God of light, Mithra, was also said to have been born on this day. Carols, gifts, feasts, and lighted trees, all originally belonged to the Nordic solstice festival of Yule, the rebirth of the sun. Going back to even earlier mythology, Christmas trees were an echo of the pine groves or *pinea silvia* which were attached to temples of the Great Mother. In France, Yule was celebrated with a festive log known as the Noel Log, originally representing the phallus of a god.

The pairing of holly and ivy dates back to the cult of Dionysus where the holly represented the feminine power and the ivy the masculinity of the god. Holly which in the Christmas carol "bears the crown" was to the druids the most sacred of trees, dedicated to the Mother Holle or Hel, Goddess of the underworld. The red berries represented her menstrual blood. Germanic witches who worshipped her used holly wood to make their magic wands.

Mistletoe, on the other hand, was considered to be the genitalia of the oak god, its white berries representing drops of semen. At sacrificial ceremonies, druid priests would castrate the oak god by cutting off his mistletoe. In fact, sacred-oak cults continued during the Christian era while in Russia, as recently as 1874, it was recorded that an ancient oak shrine was worshipped by groups under the auspices of an Orthodox priest. The ceremony was followed by a drunken orgy. The Roman historian Pliny records that the Celts set great store by the medicinal properties of the mistletoe plant and believed it to be sacred. At the time of the winter solstice they would hold a ritual, lasting a week, whose purpose was to beg the sun to be reborn. The participants, having exchanged gifts, would enjoy feasts at which they drank hot mead laced with mistletoe. Sexual orgies would follow. What remains to us today is the somewhat more restrained custom of kissing under the mistletoe.

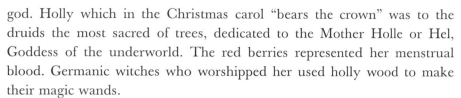

Costumes of the Druidical Order in pre-Roman Britain, c.100 BC. Both sexes were admitted to membership of the Celtic priesthood. According to the historian Strabo, their worship involved orgiastic rites.

The Celtic peoples proved particularly resistant to Christian ways. In Ireland during the twelfth century, there were complaints that the people still insisted on practicing "old, barbaric and obscene customs." Even as late as the fourteenth century the Goddess Diana was worshipped in the West of England in woodland shrines, sometimes by monks. Pagan ceremonies were largely in the hands of women, which remained the case until the twelfth and thirteenth centuries when persecution of witches became

Villagers raising the maypole. This fertility symbol survived even the most strenuous efforts of Christianity to eradicate pagan rites.

widespread. At a synod of Rome during the ninth century, it was noted that pagan worship was being carried on in churches, "Many people, mostly women, come to church on Sundays and holy days not to attend the Mass but to dance, sing bawd songs, and do other such pagan things."

As part of the effort to convert the heathen, the churches took over many shrines of the Goddess and promised that the old rites would be allowed to continue. As a result, churches throughout Europe and Great Britain are built over these shrines and other sacred mounds.

May Day, still celebrated in Europe, was originally dedicated to Maia, the Goddess of spring. In medieval times, the rite of the May King was an echo of the worship of the goddess Diana. He would fight the previous year's king and win the "queen of a magic wood," meaning the goddess. The Maypole, originally an Indian tradition, was a representation of the god's phallus being planted in the earth. At May Day festivals, the pole would be covered with flowers and bound with ribbons. The young men and women of the village would dance around it and then depart into the woods to continue with their own private celebrations in the time-honored way. Up until the sixteenth century in rural areas of Europe, May was considered a month of sexual freedom where couples, regardless of marital status, would have sex in plowed fields in order to encourage the crops to grow. Schoolchildren to this day dance around a maypole, having first crowned the May Queen. Whether or not the fond parents watching understand the symbolism of their offspring's activities is a matter for conjecture.

Gnostics

Although Gnostic cults existed before the Christian era, especially in Egypt, the term "Gnosticism" came to be used to describe the mystery cults of the early Christian era and, at a later time, the medieval heresies. Those who subscribed to the cults considered themselves to be the true Christians. They argued that their knowledge, or *gnosis*, was not something based on blind faith but was instead revealed knowledge, the result of an understanding derived from direct experience.

The information revealed in this way included insights about the true nature of God or the divine, secret information about the after life and certain words of power. For some Gnostics, the true way meant abstaining from sensual pleasures since only that which is spiritual is from God. Others, however, were decidedly in favor of sexual experience and insisted that it was good for one's spiritual development. According to this way of thinking, a man, in order to attain truth, has to live in the world and love a woman so that he is one with her. We see here a continuation of the Egyptian relationship between sex and religion which had been forced underground by the Judeo-Christian tradition. Many adherents believed in marriage for spiritual reasons but not for procreation. In early Gnosticism the central sacrament was referred to as the Bridal Chamber. Here the feminine soul of the practitioner unites with the masculine spirit, therefore becoming spiritualized.

The Gnostics focused on the feminine aspect of God, whose name was Sophia, meaning wisdom or knowledge, and who appears also in Cabbalistic literature as the *Shekhinah* or Holy Spirit of God. Sophia was usually regarded as God's female soul and sometimes as his mother. The

Trattato Gnostico of the first century AD, for instance, refers to her as, "...the great revered Virgin in whom the Father was concealed from the beginning before He had created anything." Some groups paid particular attention to Mary Magdalene, who was claimed to be the special object of Jesus's love. As pagan writings were rediscovered, there was also a renewal of interest in Isis, who appeared in various occult books as the Naked Goddess crowned with stars.

Not unsurprisingly, the orthodox church took great exception to the feminine imagery used by the Gnostics. The Church fathers were particularly offended by their custom of allowing women to take ecclesiastical rank, which finds an echo in some members of the Church of England today. Tertullian, the Carthaginian theologian and advocate, c.AD 160-220, was scandalized to hear of the women that, "...they teach, they engage in discussion; they exorcise; they cure." Even more shocking was the fact that women were allowed to perform the rites of baptism. Yet in spite of tireless persecution by the orthodox churches, secret Gnostic societies flourished for centuries. Cult objects have been found in Sicily, Spain and Southern France, particularly sacred boxes knows as *coffretes gnostiques*.

Many Gnostic Christians practiced the *agape*, or love feast. These took different forms but would usually involve group sexual activity, after which semen and menstrual blood would be consumed. As the living substances of reproduction, they were considered to be more spiritually potent than the bread and wine of the conventional Eucharist. The Gnostics were not alone in this view since semen and menstrual blood also feature in occult Tantric rites. One outraged commentator, Epiphanius, c.AD 315-413, has left us an account from the *agape* as practiced by a sect known as the Ophites in *The Panarion*:

> *"The women they share in common... When they extend their hands, apparently in greeting, they tickle the other's palm in a certain way and so discover whether the new arrival belongs to their cult... Husbands separate from their wives, and a man will say to his own spouse, 'Arise and celebrate the love feast with thy brother.' And the wretches mingle with each other... after they have consorted together in a passionate debauch... The woman and the man take the man's ejaculation into their hands, stand up... offering to the Father, the Primal Being of All Nature, what is on their hands, with the words, 'We bring to Thee this oblation, which is the very Body of Christ.' ... They consume it... And when the woman is in her period, they*

Mary Magdalene, who has been identified since the earliest times with the sinning woman who anointed the Lord's feet.

OPPOSITE: *Mary Madgalen and Bishop Teobaldo Pontano.* The Magdalen Chapel, Assissi. School of Giotto.

do likewise with her menstruation. The unclean flow of blood, which they garner, they take up in the same way and eat together. And that, they say is Christ's Blood. For when they read in Revelation, 'I saw the tree of life with its twelve kinds of fruit, yielding its fruit each month,' they interpret this as an allusion to the monthly incidence of the female period."

Contemporary wife (and husband) swapping parties certainly pale into total insignificance in comparison to these rituals of long ago.

In complete contrast, many Gnostics considered matter to be inherently evil as is evidenced by texts, such as the Gospel of Thomas, which are decidedly ascetic in tone. This view greatly offended St. Paul who, in his first letter to Timothy, refers to "doctrines of devils" whose followers are forbidden to marry and must abstain from eating meat. In the second century AD, Marcion rejected the notion of God as a stern lawgiver and judge, the Jehovah of the Old Testament. The true God, he declared, was the God of Love as revealed by Jesus. But in his view, this was a love which was purely spiritual. Marriage and procreation were therefore considered to be the work of Satan and accordingly condemned.

Towards the end of the third century, Manichaeism arrived in the West from its home in Persia, where it had been proclaimed at the court of the Persian king Shahpur I by the prophet, Manichaeus or Mani, around AD 245. This was a philosophy of extreme dualism whereby there were two basic aspects of the universe, namely God and matter. God was the source of everything which was good, whereas matter, alias the Devil, was intrinsically evil. Matter, we should perhaps not be surprised to learn, was considered female and said to imprison the soul. Since the purpose of Manichaeism was to set free the soul, an extreme degree of asceticism had to be practiced. This religion was evidently very appealing, for it spread rapidly, eventually as far as Rome and North Africa.

Courtly Love

In France, until the time of the Crusades, an upperclass woman was regarded by her menfolk more or less as a possession. Initially she belonged to her father who would dispose of her in marriage as he saw fit. Her role was that of a pawn in the game of acquiring money, property, power. She then became the responsibility of her husband whom she was naturally required to present with heirs. Should he die, she would be dependent for her well-being on her sons. Her job was to obey the men and not cause trouble.

Then, around the beginning of the twelfth century, came the Crusades. Men left in droves for the Holy Land, leaving their wives to take responsibility for the management of affairs at home. This marked a turning point in the position of women who had formerly been powerless to influence their destiny. Now they began to think for themselves, to exercise authority and make decisions, as they moved for the first time beyond the purely domestic realm into a wider world. Their new status must have created an extraordinary change in the way women perceived themselves and were, in turn, perceived by men. Freed from the constraints of domesticity and submissiveness to a man's will, they would undoubtedly have acquired a much greater degree of self-respect. And this, we know, engenders the respect of others, the others in this case being men.

Largely as a result of this change of attitude towards women, there now developed the phenomenon known as courtly love. Under the auspices of Eleanor of Aquitaine, it began as a game with complex rules, developed as a pastime enabling bored aristocrats to while away their endless hours of leisure. For the first time, we meet the theme of the devoted knight who worships his lady as a goddess. Here is perhaps the beginning of the romantic myth underlying Western notions of relationship to this day, the fairy story to be realized in life. Back in the twelfth century, it was more a case of "while the husband's away, the lady will play."

Although according to the strict rules of the game, the knight's love had to remain unrequited, courtly love was essentially adulterous. This makes sense when we consider

LEFT: The formidable Queen Eleanor of Aquitaine, Queen Consort of France and subsequently also of England.

BELOW: Troubadors shown playing a game of chess - or is it a game of Love? From a 14th century ivory plaque.

The Tournament Prize. Only knights of unblemished character were allowed to exhibit their courage and skill in combat. From *The Tournaments of King Réné*, 15th century.

that love and marriage quite definitely did not go together at this time. Marriage was simply a business transaction in which love played no part. A knight would choose as the object of his devotion a lady who was married and therefore, at least in theory, unattainable. In order to win her love, he had to strive to become worthy of her. He must give unquestioning obedience to her every wish without any expectation of being rewarded. If he were lucky, she might consent to a secret meeting, perhaps a kiss. Whether she chose to bestow further favors on him was entirely up to the lady in question. A most revolutionary idea was being proposed, at least in terms of Judeo-Christian culture, namely that a women might be free to choose a lover.

Hand-in-hand with the convention of courtly love went the phenomenon of the troubadours. Originating in Provence, they later spread elsewhere into France and into Germany, where they were known as *Minnesingers*, or singers of love. The tradition had actually begun a few hundred years earlier, in the harem culture of the Near East. Poets and storytellers, inspired by the mysterious qualities of the ladies concealed within the harem, would write love songs in their honor. A poet would dedicate his work to a particular lady, obviously unattainable and therefore largely a figment of his imagination. The feelings involved were thought to be a pure form of love, as opposed to sex. Once the pilgrims and Crusaders had come into contact with Arabian culture, it was only a matter of time before this custom of enshrining a pure love into song made its way into France.

Several of the more distinguished troubadours benefited from the patronage of Eleanor of Aquitaine, a lady ahead of her time. These were the first writers of romantic songs, usually written around the theme of a knight who falls in love with a great lady, struggles to make himself worthy of her and eventually wins her love. The troubadour tradition understood love in terms of a divine visitation involving an intense person-to-person relationship, a revolutionary idea at the time. They considered this form of relationship infinitely more spiritual than marriage, which was arranged and ordered by society, usually for materially advantageous reasons. Marriage was viewed as a form of spiritual adultery since it was merely an arrangement, having nothing to do with the meeting of two souls. Not surprisingly, this was held to be a heretical view. Love, for the troubadours, was the meaning of life itself, a view which permeated romances such as the story of Tristan and Isolde. Although Isolde had never met him, she was engaged to be married to King Mark of Cornwall. He sends Tristan to escort her to his kingdom and the two fall in love, in other words making the true marriage which, being socially unacceptable, leads to tragedy.

Sex and Heresy: Cathars and Templars

Along with the flowering of courtly love there developed in the area of France known as the Languedoc the phenomenon of Catharism. The Cathars, sometimes called the Albigensians, after the town of Albi, one of their main centers, had much in common with early Gnostic groups. They were a heretical sect who rejected the Catholic Church, insisted on direct knowledge of God and subscribed to a doctrine of reincarnation. Women were allowed to teach, to preach and to take lovers. Indeed, extramarital sex, based on love and affection, was considered infinitely preferable to the dutiful variety practiced within a marriage based on considerations of property and inheritance. True love between two freely consenting people could even serve to purify those involved from the false "love" of the marriage bed.

For the Cathars it was not sex but procreation which was sinful. They believed that the material world was an evil creation. Only the world of the spirit could, in their eyes, be entirely good. Incarnation was therefore held to be a sin and a punishment for past transgressions. To produce children would be to give yet further support to the world of matter, thereby lending power to the spirit of evil. The ultimate goal was to unite with the spirit of pure love, which they held to be the true God. Loving sex symbolized this union and was perhaps the closest you were likely to get to heaven on earth.

The story of a certain weaver of Toulouse named John demonstrates the absolute difference between what the Roman church considered a devout way of life and the Cathar viewpoint. Having been accused of subscribing to the Gnostic heresy, John declared that he lied, swore, ate meat, and enjoyed sex with his wife. This, he contended, proved his credentials as a faithful Christian, not a heretic.

Although the Cathars have acquired a reputation for sexual abstinence, this is a distortion of the truth. The teachers and preachers, men and women known as *parfaits* or "perfected ones," did indeed take vows of chastity as part of their quest for enlightenment. Their spiritual path entailed avoiding any identification with the world of matter and therefore of flesh. But the *parfaits* were a minority of those involved in the Cathar movement and far too realistic to try and impose their own practices on the ordinary followers.

To avoid procreation, the Cathars are thought to have practiced both birth control and abortion. When the Church of Rome decided, not altogether unsurprisingly, that such a dangerous form of heresy had to be wiped out, the heretics were accused, among many other things, of "unnatural sexual practices." This was generally assumed to refer to sodomy. After all, the reasoning went, these people not only held un-Christian views about sex but also condemned procreation. Which could surely only mean that they practiced either homosexuality or heterosexual anal intercourse as a way of avoiding conception. Such records as survive suggest that the Cathars were, on the contrary, very much against homosexuality. Doubtless the fact that the *parfaits* were accustomed to travel around the countryside in pairs added weight to these rumors.

A much earlier movement known as the Manichaean heresy had become strongly established in southern France and made links with similar sects in Bulgaria. Its followers were

Relief of a *Christ Crucified*, or perhaps in prayer, at the church at Les Casses, France. It is said to be a gravestone, reminiscent of the heretical Bogomil images, and now linked with the Cathars.

referred to as Bulgars or Bougres, terms which became synonymous with heresy. Once the purges of the Church began, the Cathars also were identified as Bougres. Given the assumptions which were made about their sexual proclivities, it is not difficult to see how the term "buggery" came into being.

Homosexual intercourse had been deemed a form of heresy from around the beginning of the twelfth century. It subsequently became linked to witchcraft through the belief that participants in ceremonial witchcraft were required to kiss the buttocks or anus of a human or perhaps an animal. Official status was granted to the notion of the practice of the "obscene kiss" as it was called, in a Papal bull issued in 1233. This document, based on the statement of an inquisitor, claimed that groups of heretics held secret meetings in which prospective members of the sect had to kiss the devil on the mouth or anus. The devil might appear in the form of a black cat, a toad, goose or duck, or even as a thin man with black and shining eyes.

Some versions of the "obscene kiss" were theatrical in the extreme. One group of Albigensians were held to practice their secret rituals in a cave. During the ceremony the so-called "bishop" of the sect would bare his buttocks and insert a silver spoon into his anus. Upon this an offering was made. Each member of the congregation then kissed the bishop's proffered backside before gathering round a pillar to which clung a huge cat. The feline anus had then also to be kissed. Finally all present joined in a communal embrace, men with men, and women with other women. This sect, it was claimed, taught that while marriage involved the sin of fornication, sodomy was a perfectly acceptable expression of sexuality.

Perhaps the best-known attempt to equate unorthodox forms of sexual expression with the sin of heresy was in the trial of the Knights Templar. A crusading order founded at the beginning of the twelfth century to protect pilgrims to the Holy Land, its adherents adopted vows of poverty and chastity. Only knights of noble birth were admitted into the highest class of Templars, whose duty was to fight for Christianity. Over a period of years, the order became very rich. Donations were plentiful and pilgrims on their way to the Holy Land often entrusted their valuables to the Knights in return for a note which could be redeemed once they arrived in Palestine. The Templars, who appear to have been extremely honest, were in effect used as bankers and in due course were in a position to lend large sums of money. Among those taking advantage of their financial services were the kings of France. By now the Templars were therefore able to wield considerable financial influence throughout much of Europe to the extent that, for a time, the head of the order appeared to have as much power as any of the royal monarchs. Doubtless this was a major contributory factor leading to their downfall.

On the night of October 13, 1307, Philip IV of France ordered all the

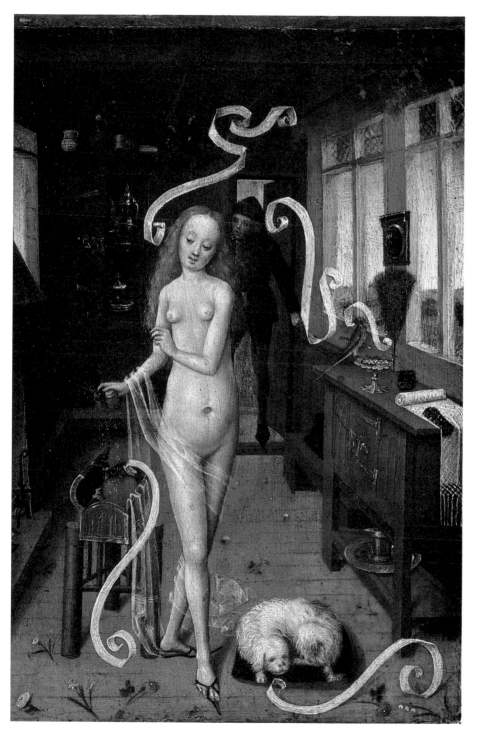

The Sorceress, from a painting by Georgi-Dmitroff Platzi, 16th century. She appears to be making elaborate preparation for a rite of sex magic, perhaps with the man entering the room.

Templars in his land to be arrested and charged with heresy and sodomy. One of the many charges laid at their door concerned rituals which took place during the initiation ceremony. It was alleged that the Templars had to kiss the official who received them on the buttock, navel or penis, and the mouth. Having done this, they were informed that they were free to copulate with each other and that, if another Templar required them to do so, they must submit passively. The seriousness of the crime of sodomy may be inferred from the fact that although many of the Templars confessed to spitting on the cross, an activity also claimed to be part of the initiation ceremony, hardly any would admit to taking part in homosexual practices.

Indeed, the sin of sodomy appears to have been an obsession of the medieval mind. Even Dante, one of the most humane figures of the Renaissance, classifies several of his contemporaries, including well-known literary figures, as "sodomists" who are, as a result, to be found in the seventh level of the Inferno, taking their punishment. Interestingly, Julius Caesar is also mentioned as a sodomite but he is placed in purgatory rather than hell, for reasons which are not at all clear.

From Heresy to Witchcraft

Towards the end of the Middle Ages, sorcery and witchcraft replaced heresy as a focus of major concern. During the thirteenth century, heresy and sorcery began to be bracketed together. Two hundred years later, sorcerers and witches would be punished even though they were no longer charged with heresy as well. The Inquisition, having apparently succeeded in its original brief of crushing heresy, now needed further employment, to which end it turned its attention to all forms of sorcery. Between 1431 and 1447, Pope Eugenius IV defined the crimes of magic and sorcery in terms of classical witchcraft and ordered the Inquisition to proceed against their perpetrators. But it was in 1484 that the most important Papal bull against witchery was published by Innocent VIII. Here it was stated that:

"... it has come to our ears that members of both sexes do not avoid to have intercourse with demons, incubi and succubi; and that by their sorceries and by their incantation, charms and conjurations, they suffocate, extinguish and cause to perish the births of women, the increase of animals, the corn of the ground, the grapes of the vineyard and the fruit of the trees, as well as men, women, flocks, herbs and

Witches by Baldung

other various kinds of animals, vines and apple trees, corn and other fruits of the earth; making and procuring that men and women, flocks and herds and other animals shall suffer and be tormented both from within and without so that men beget not nor women conceive; and they impede the conjugal action of men and women."

In 1486, this bull appeared as the preface to the *Malleus Maleficarum*, or *The Hammer of Witches*, the handbook for all future witch-hunters. The appearance of this work heralded the major onset of the witch craze, which reached its height in about 1600 and was not finally to end until the eighteenth century. Witchcraft was defined as the most abominable of heresies, involving the devotion of the body and soul to evil and sexual relations with incubi or succubi. These creatures were the manifestations of demons who would assume human form, incubi being the male, and succubi the female, for the purpose of intercourse with humans. Technically they were defined as angels who, owing to their lustful desires, had fallen from their heavenly status. Since they were credited with being able to change sex at will, intercourse with them might well involve their human

Witches flying up a chimney on their broomsticks, 1597.

partner also in some kind of transsexual change. And because they belonged by definition to a species different from the human, such intercourse could be condemned as bestiality or buggery. In their zeal to prove such cases, witch-hunters gathered many accounts of monsters, strange and weird beings, half human and half animal, which were ostensibly the products of these unions.

One problem which greatly interested theologians was how to explain the fact that an incubus could have organs which resembled those of

The Four Witches, from an engraving by Dürer, 1497. Witchcraft was the survival of the pre-Christian fertility religions whose gods were condemned as devils by the Church.

humans and could emit semen. A thirteenth-century authority on the matter claimed that the incubi operated a kind of transcendental semen collection service. They would gather the human semen emitted either during nocturnal emissions or as a result of masturbation and use it to create new bodies for themselves. Other experts, following the lead of St. Thomas Aquinas, contended that the demons, in the guise of succubi, seduced males and received their semen. Subsequently they would take on the role of incubi, enabling them to pour this semen into the female recipient. Incubi, it was noted, greatly outnumbered succubi, the reason being that women were, as usual, considered far more licentious than men and therefore far more attractive to demons. Indeed, official handbooks for inquisitors declared that witchcraft and Satanism were caused by women's "carnal lust," since God "allows the devil more power over the venereal act, by which the original sin is handed down, than over all other human actions...because of its natural nastiness."

Another topic of great interest to those involved was the size of an incubus's penis. Most men at this time were under the illusion that penis size was directly related to ability as a lover. One authority declared that women who consorted with incubi subsequently discovered that the efforts of a mere man were "paltry and unable to arouse them to any degree." An accused witch reported that the devil had "a member like a mule's, having chosen to imitate that animal as being best endowed by nature; that it was as long and as thick as an arm.....and that he always exposed his instrument, of such beautiful shape and measurements."

The word "witch" itself derives from the Anglo-Saxon "wicca," meaning a seer or diviner. The original practitioners of witchcraft were predominantly women who worshipped the Great Goddess and practiced the healing arts using their considerable knowledge of herbs. Indeed, up to the fifteenth century, theirs was virtually the only medicine available, given that the Church believed sickness to be the result of demonic possession and therefore curable only by exorcism. As late as 1570 a witch was released from her prison in Canterbury Castle on the grounds that her homely remedies were more effective for the sick than all the prayers and exorcisms of the local priest.

Witchcraft was more or less allowed up until the fourteenth century. Witches would often be employed by nobility and even the clergy in a healing capacity or perhaps to raise a thunderstorm, which it was thought

they could do at will, and was useful in dispersing enemy armies. However, the Church eventually decided that these manifestations of feminine power were unacceptable and denounced the craft as a heresy. From then on, the Church would propagate the idea that witches were the helpers of the Devil and persecute them accordingly. War was declared on female healers and women were forbidden to study medicine.

Myths about the witches' lifestyle became legion: they brewed up magic potions in cauldrons, kept cats as familiars, and were in the habit of sticking pins into wax dolls. And if there is one thing every child knows about a witch it is that she flies around on a broomstick. This tradition originates in the pagan feminine mystery rites concerning marriage and birth where a broomstick would play an important part. In Rome the broom was the symbol of a priestess-midwife, and of Hecate, the goddess who also presided over marriage, so that the broom symbolized sexual union. Old wedding customs, in the times before the Church took charge of nuptial rites, included jumping over a broomstick, perhaps to represent impregnation. The connection with the phallus is of course obvious, riding the broomstick signifying the sexual position where the woman is on top, a position considered by the medieval Church to be a perversion.

A nursery rhyme sung by countless generations of children was in fact a witch-rhyme:

"Ride a cock-horse to Banbury Cross
To see a fine lady ride on a white horse."

The fine lady in question was Godiva, originally a Gothic Goddess. She later found fame in her incarnation as Lady Godiva who rode naked through the town of Coventry on a white horse annually until 1826 when it was decreed that she must wear clothes. In an echo of the original May-Eve procession of the Goddess, the purpose of the ride was to consummate the sacred marriage with her consort, represented by the horse, ensuring fertility for the coming year.

Witches were also famous for flying through the air at night, with or without a broomstick. Certain French witches are known to have used a dildo anointed with what was called flying ointment. This was probably aconite or perhaps a mixture of hallucinogenic substances such as hemlock, mandrake, and belladonna, all associated with witchcraft. According to the Inquisition, a possible destination of the night flight, in which witches

Lady Godiva preparing to leave her husband's home and ride naked through the streets of Coventry, in order to persuade him to reduce the excessive rates of taxes levied on the townspeople. After an engraving by J.B. Allen, 1852.

would be accompanied by the pagan Goddess Diana, was the Sabbat. Here perverted rituals would be practiced, such as kissing the devil's anus, drinking menstrual blood and indulging in generally licentious and therefore un-Christian behavior. The Witches' Sabbat was in fact almost entirely a fiction invented by the Inquisition. Witches certainly confessed to such "crimes" but this is hardly surprising given the nature of the torture to which they were subjected.

If all women were susceptible to sexual enticement by the devil then none were considered more vulnerable than nuns. At one convent in Cologne the devil, in the form of a dog, was said to lift up the robes of nuns in order to abuse them. Perhaps as a result of the church's teaching that nuns were brides of Christ, some claimed that they had slept with their heavenly husband. Perhaps illogically, under the circumstances, such claims were condemned as blasphemous and held to be the result of demonic possession.

One of the most notorious cases concerning nuns occurred in the seventeenth century at Loudun, in France. A priest, Urbain Grandier, had openly ignored his vows of celibacy, relying on his political connections to protect him. Several of his opponents, determined to bring about his downfall, hatched a plot involving some of the sisters of the Ursuline convent. The nuns were persuaded to swear that they were possessed as a result of having been bewitched by Father Grandier. The Mother Superior, Sister Jeanne des Anges, and one of the nuns added credibility to the accusation by going into convulsions, holding their breath until their bodies swelled, and altering their looks and voices. These initial efforts having failed to prevent Father Grandier's activities, the plot was extended. Exorcisms were carried out, as a result of which about sixty witnesses testified to adultery, incest, sacrilege and other sexual crimes committed by the priest. Typical of the nuns' conduct under exorcism was the behavior of a young nun, Sister Claire:

> "She fell on the ground, blaspheming, in convulsions, lifting up her petticoats and chemise, displaying her privy parts without any shame, and uttering filthy words. Her gestures became so indecent that the audience averted its eyes. She cried out again and again, abusing herself with her hands, 'Come on, then, foutez-moi (screw me).'"

A considerable amount of damning evidence was manufactured against

Father Grandier. Although several nuns later tried to retract their confessions, the courts refused to allow this on the grounds that their change of mind had been arranged by the Devil to save his servant. Grandier was convicted of causing demoniacal possession of several Ursuline nuns and was subsequently tortured to death while being burned.

Witchcraft and sorcery were also held to be responsible for impotence, infertility and many activities connected with sex. A witch might, for example, prevent a woman from conceiving or cause her to miscarry. Among other supposed powers of a witch was her ability to make a man's penis disappear by casting a "glamor" over it. Once this happened, only the witch herself was able to make it reappear. A witch might also be regarded as the main cause of a man's failure to achieve an erection, while impotence was believed to be the result of a ligature she had made. By tying knots in threads or hanks of leather, she supposedly rendered the man sexually incapable until the hidden knot was discovered or untied, or until the witch lifted her spell. By and large, however, believers in witchcraft thought that the devil was more interested in encouraging than preventing fornication and so ligature was held to be less common than the other forms of *malefica*, or evils, that a witch might impose.

Because of the magical properties thought to be associated with hair, the inquisitors would shave the hair of accused witches before torturing them. In this way, they would lose the protection of Satan. Where male witches were concerned, body hair might also be shaved. Since this preceded confession, usually as a result of torture, it became the origin of the phrase "to make a clean breast of things."

It is impossible to say how many people were executed as witches in Europe during the period of persecution from 1450 to 1750, since records are incomplete. Some authorities estimate that millions were beheaded, hanged, whipped to death, or burned alive. Nor was the persecution of witches confined to Europe. In 1692 the famous witch trials at Salem, Massachusetts, were the starting point of a witchhunting mania which spread throughout the state. Over four hundred people were accused of witchcraft, many of whom died while awaiting trial in cold, damp cells. In Salem alone, nineteen were found guilty and hanged. Ironically, in 1693 reason finally prevailed, the jurors at Salem repented of their actions and humbly begged the forgiveness of those they had harmed – far too late in the day for some.

CHAPTER 6

The Scientific Breakthrough

Anatomical Knowledge: Myths Old and New

T HE PERIOD BETWEEN THE SIXTEENTH and nineteenth centuries saw a growing interest in sexual anatomy and procreation. Some of the beliefs about these subjects had not materially changed since ancient Greek times. Aristotle, in the fourth century BC had reached the conclusion that the female sexual organs were similar to those of the male but that hers were inside the body. She was, as it were, an imperfect variety of male which had not managed to emerge into the light of day. As far as conception was concerned, while the man contributed semen to the process, the woman provided menstrual blood as the passive material for the semen to work on. Aristotle thought that a small penis was to be preferred as the semen in a larger one would be colder and therefore less potent. This must have been a widespread belief as in Greek art, it is usually only satyrs who are depicted as being sexually well-endowed, the preferred mode for men being small and delicate.

Aristotle's thought was developed by the second-century Greek

"That'S Phyllis .....that was." A poster warning the Allied troops in Italy, 1943-44, of the dangers of venereal disease.

171

physician, Soranus. He reasoned that since the woman's penis was hidden on the inside of her body, the vagina was therefore its foreskin, which grew around the neck of the womb in the same way as the foreskin around the glans. At around the same time, Galen developed his theory that the retention of the sexual organs within the woman's body was due to a lack of vital heat. Galen was also convinced that women produced semen, although it was naturally inferior to that of the man. Hippocrates held not dissimilar views, declaring that each partner produced a germinal substance, a kind of sperm which blended. Although the ovaries were discovered at the beginning of the Christian era, they were held to be the female and therefore inferior version of the testicles, producing a poorer quality of semen,

A few hundred years later, a fourth-century bishop agreed that women's sexual organs were like those of a man except that they were inside the body. Variations of this view were to remain current until the Middle Ages. Renaissance anatomists, in their illustrations of the sexual organs, clearly demonstrated their belief that the vagina was a kind of inverted penis. Not until the eighteenth century was the uterus defined and the female organs given the names as we know now them. By this time the myth of woman as an inferior being both sexually and intellectually was deeply entrenched in the collective psyche. So strong was this belief that it remained influential right up to the time of Freud and provided the basis for his theories.

In due course, the Church fathers developed Aristotle's proposal that the active ingredient in conception was semen. Clement of Alexandria believed it to be a substance which was "almost man," while St. Thomas Aquinas declared that the woman was simply the passive vehicle enabling the child to come to birth. In his view, since woman's existence was on an altogether lower plane than that of a man, a female child was necessarily the result of a flawed process. His teachings were, alas, to prove a decisive influence in Catholic theology. Not until the middle of the seventeenth century was it discovered that semen contained sperm. Antony van Leeuwenhoeck, when examining some seminal fluid under a microscope in 1675, found that it contained what he called "animalcules." In true chauvinist fashion, he decided that these were miniature humans for whom the woman's egg merely provided a nest in which they could grow to birth-size. It took until the middle of the nineteenth century for the true nature of the role of egg and sperm to be discovered.

Renaissance doctors attributed women's diseases to the fact that the womb would detach itself and wander around inside the body. This, they said, gave rise to uncontrolled emotional behavior which they called "hysteria," from the Greek word for womb. Possibly they did not know that *Hysteria* was originally the name given to a religious festival held in honor of the goddess Aphrodite where orgiastic rites took place with the purpose of celebrating and fertilizing the Womb of the World.

In 1559 a man named Columbus, an explorer of anatomy, claimed to have discovered the clitoris, which he believed to be a female penis. Since for many centuries, no virtuous woman would dream of revealing her naked body even to her husband, physicians had little opportunity to check their anatomical facts. Many even believed that a devout woman would by definition have no clitoris. Greek mythology again provides the origin of the name for this part of the female anatomy. The word *kleitoris* means divine, or goddess-like, after an Amazon queen called Kleite. In another legend Kleite was a nymph who loved the phallus of the sun god and would follow its movement with her head, a clearly sexual image. This myth in fact comes far closer to the truth of how female sexuality functions than do any of the theories proposed much before the twentieth century.

A marble head of Aristotle, the Greek philosopher, an early explorer of sexual anatomy, 384-322 BC.

Marriage Changes

We have seen how thoroughly goddess worship, with its emphasis on feminine values, was stamped out by the Church in Europe. Nowhere were the effects of this more evident than in the development of marriage. The patriarchal values of Jehovah and Judaism returned with a vengeance and, at least where marriage was concerned, held far greater sway than the idea of forgiveness of sins proposed by Christ.

Since ancient times, marriage had been mainly the concern of the upper classes who had fortunes and estates to consider and would therefore need a formal contract to safeguard their interests. For those lower down the social scale, there was a type of informal, common-law marriage, based simply on cohabitation and unmarked by any special ceremony. The couple were free to terminate the relationship at any time. Trial marriages, often of a temporary nature, were legal in Europe up to the early years of the seventeenth century. Among the peasant classes, a betrothal would often mean nothing more than that the young couple were allowed to spend nights together. If the girl became pregnant as a result, she would not necessarily marry the man in question. Illegitimacy was widespread throughout all classes of medieval society.

Because sacred marriage had been associated with goddess-worship, there was no possibility of wedlock being sanctified by the early Christian Church. On the contrary, once the Church fathers had decided that celibacy was the most blessed state, marriage was considered a sin. Until the later Middle Ages, it therefore came within the jurisdiction of the common law. Churchmen were, in fact, in something of a quandary about the whole issue. In spite of the early rule of celibacy for clergy, priests had begun to marry during the fifth and sixth centuries. This they continued to do until the papal decrees of the eleventh century which required them to get rid of their wives and sell their children as slaves. The reasoning behind this draconian measure was purely economic. If priests could no longer leave their property to their offspring, they had no option but to bequeath it to the Church. Secret marriages nevertheless took place, including that of Thomas Cranmer, created Archbishop of Canterbury in 1532. In 1559, after the Reformation, Church authorities finally capitulated and priests of the Protestant church were legally allowed to marry. After that marriage became a sacrament.

Even this progressive step did little to lessen the dualism of flesh and spirit. The Church still remained averse to sex and women. From 1549 onwards, three reasons for getting married were specifically named in the marriage service. Although primarily for the procreation of children, the marital state served also as "a remedy against sin, and to avoid fornication; that such persons as have not the gift of continency might marry, and keep themselves undefiled." A wife must promise to obey her husband and although he is told to honor her, this was solely on the basis that she is the weaker vessel and not as an equal partner.

The service of baptism declared that "all men are conceived and born in sin" – implying that even marital sex was not spiritually acceptable. Consequently, from medieval times onwards, it was accepted that a virtuous woman did not experience sex as pleasurable but as something she

was obliged to endure for the sake of procreation. Since nakedness was most decidedly not a sign of virtue, a very devout married couple would wear large nightgowns to bed, each having a small hole judiciously placed in the front to allow penetration.

Marriage was not formally adopted as a Christian sacrament until 1563. Having at last decided to bestow its official approval the Church, in its usual all-encompassing fashion, decided to make itself necessary for anyone wishing to enter the marital state. It declared that what constituted a marriage was the blessing of a priest. Common-law unions were no longer recognized as such, at least by the Church hierarchy. In 1753, a blessing in church was finally made a formal legal requirement in England. Matters were different in Scotland, however. Here it was still possible for a couple to be legally wedded simply by having their hands joined in the presence of witnesses. The resulting phenomenon of elopement across the border to Gretna Green lasted well into the twentieth century.

Once the Church had reluctantly given its approval to marriage, it was

The famous Smithy at Gretna Green, Dumfries, Scotland, which has for many years proclaimed that over 10,000 marriages have been performed in this room. It was the traditional haven of runaway couples from England.

not slow to take every advantage of that fact. When she married, a woman's property was taken from her and given to her husband, who for all intents and purposes, owned her. Men were constantly reminded, in the unlikely event that they had forgotten, that women were sinners. They were therefore exhorted by the Church to discipline their wives and make them obedient unto them, the result being that wife-beating became commonplace. Many women, having no means of supporting themselves, were forced unwillingly into wedlock rather than remain spinsters dependent on the largesse of their family.

At the beginning of the seventeenth century attitudes in the Christian church began to change. With the Reformation and Counter-Reformation, the seeds of rationalist philosophy had been sown. The reformers saw celibacy as a contravention of the divine law. Luther, the German religious reformer, 1483-1546, thought chastity both abnormal and undesirable and dismissed the idea that virginity was to be glorified, a view which he held in common with the Hebrew patriarchs. Like them, he believed that marriage was necessary to human nature and that a man needed a wife as a companion and support. Nor did he think the idea of marriage for life could be justified, particularly in cases of adultery and desertion. For Luther, Christ's view that separation was only possible provided there was no remarriage was an ideal to be aimed for rather than an absolute obligation. Nor did he believe that marriage was a specifically Christian sacrament, given that it had been founded long before the Church came into existence. He therefore saw it as a purely secular arrangement and, to prove the point, was married to a former nun in 1525, in his own home.

Martin Luther, depicted in the broadsheet of his *Farewell to the World*. Luther turned upside down many of the traditional Catholic views about sexuality and marriage.

Calvin, the French Protestant reformer, 1509-64, went even further and declared that marital sex was something holy and honorable. Marriage was not simply for procreation. It had equal importance as a social relationship in which the couple are meant to be true companions. Nevertheless, he agreed with Luther that women, on account of their inferiority, should be subject to the authority of their menfolk. Nothing, it seemed, would overturn this particular myth.

Puritans and Patriarchs

In England the Puritan movement began early in the reign of Queen Elizabeth I, 1558-1603. Early Puritans thought the Church of England both too Catholic and too political, as a result of which many chose to emigrate to New England in order to enjoy religious freedom. Their attitudes to sex, marriage, and everything else were informed by the belief in original sin. The fight against inborn weakness demanded constant self-examination and self-discipline, together with unremitting hard work. Marital sex, since it had in their view been ordained by God, was not frowned upon. The extramarital variety was not even to be thought of. Families were run along the most sternly patriarchal lines, as is evidenced by group portraits of the time, joyless faces staring sternly out from the canvas.

Nothing could be allowed to undermine the institution of the family and fornicators and adulterers were therefore subjected to flogging as a deterrent. Wives also came in for their share of beating, a tradition which continued to influence family life well into the nineteenth century. In 1777, Abigail Adams wrote to her husband John on the subject, when he was helping to draw up the constitution of the United States. "Do not put such unlimited power in the hands of husbands. Remember, all men would be tyrants if they could," she pleaded. Alas, her wishes were not taken into account. For the Puritans, a husband "exercised the authority of God" over his wife, a view with which his spouse was expected to agree. And women, by now thoroughly brainwashed into the myth of masculine supremacy, did acquiesce. The theme of women submitting to their husband's dominance was later echoed by Emily Post in her book *Etiquette*, where she describes the instincts of a lady. "As an unhappy wife, her dignity demands that she never show her disapproval of her husband, no matter how publicly he slights or outrages her."

A Puritan family. Note how the husband commands the attention of his wife and children who sit, submissively, waiting his word.

Rakes Galore

In England, the inevitable reaction against Puritanism duly began to take hold. With the restoration of Charles II in 1660 came a relaxation of moral attitudes, symbolized by a brighter, more elaborate style of dress and longer hair. The King himself set the tone in terms of sexual behavior. Sexually voracious, he acquired a string of mistresses, including the commoner Nell Gwynne, and a large brood of illegitimate children. A quite different myth was now beginning to inform collective behavior, a Bacchic spirit which grew to its fullness in the eighteenth century. Drink was perhaps the principal indulgence of this era, closely followed by sexual permissiveness. Rowdy men, with nothing to do but enjoy themselves as they pleased, gathered to drink and dine at their clubs, subsequently adjourning to a theater or a brothel to round off the evening's entertainment. Nobody expected a man to prefer the company of his wife, who would often alleviate her boredom by discreetly taking a lover.

London at this time was home to a very great number of brothels, ranging from extremely grand and well-appointed houses to lowly taverns. Most were very well-advertised. Each year, a certain Mr. Harris, evidently an entrepreneurial soul, published the *Harris' List of Covent Garden Ladies*. In this were detailed the physical attributes and accomplishments of all the better-known ladies of pleasure in the area. So successful was his enterprise that he followed it up with a similar guide to the ladies of Piccadilly. Some brothels, such as that belonging to one Mrs. Goadsby, were highly exclusive. Having visited equivalent French establishments, this lady decided to run her own along the lines of a salon. After the theater, clients would assemble in the drawing room where excellent food and drink was provided, and a choice of girls of high quality, more in the style of the Greek *hetaera*. Highly professional, Mrs. Goadsby's girls were subject to strict rules particularly in respect to drinking.

Some years earlier, at the end of the seventeenth century, a club had been founded called *The Dancing Club*. The dancing here was wild and frenzied, in the manner of a Bacchanalian orgy, and a prelude to all sorts of sexual activity provided by the many prostitutes who made the club their base. Ladies farther up the social scale attended fancy-dress balls where they vied with each other to see who could be the most scantily clad. One aristocratic lady left to posterity an account of the costume worn by a Miss Chudleigh:

"Miss Chudleigh's dress, or rather, undress, was very interesting. She represented Iphigenia before her Sacrifice *but she was so unclothed that the High Priest had no difficulty at all in closely examining the victim. The ladies, who themselves were not too strait-laced, were so revolted at this that they refused to speak to her."*

An engraving of Sir Francis Dashwood dressed as a monk, kneeling in a cave and worshipping a figure of Venus.

Certain wealthy men of the time did not deign to visit brothels but kept their own private harems or, failing that, held regular orgies in their homes. One of the most notorious rakes of the eighteenth century was Sir Francis Dashwood who, from an early age, had acquired an unparalleled reputation for debauchery. At Medmenham, the home of his friend, Francis Duffield, which he had lavishly decorated in highly indecent fashion, Sir Francis held orgies which acquired an almost mythical status. In the ruins of the adjoining abbey, he and his aristocratic cronies practiced Satanism, referring to themselves as "friars." Sir Francis was reputed to have an intimate acquaintance with all the best-known whores in London, many of whom attended the Medmenham orgies for the benefit of the friars and who were consequently referred to as "nuns." In due course, Medmenham attracted unwelcome public attention and Sir Francis moved his center of operations to his house at West Wycombe. Conveniently located within his grounds was a series of caves, the perfect underground cover for the activities of his *Hell-Fire Club*, whose members could indulge themselves undisturbed. The caves are still in existence and open to visitors, a fascinating reminder of a legendary man.

The Victorian Era: Ignorance and Hypocrisy

Throughout history, the collective approach to sexuality tends to operate in a cycle of action and reaction. A period of permissiveness will almost inevitably be followed by one of repression. True to form, eighteenth-century excesses gave way to Victorian prudery. In studying Victorian attitudes to sex and the peculiar myths which accompanied them, we are dealing with a belief-system which was predominantly middle-class. Both working class and aristocracy continued in their own way, much as before, paying little heed to what others might think. If the upper classes followed anybody at this time, it was the Prince of Wales, with his taste for high living and sexual adventures with glamorous women such as the actress, Lily Langtry. In the great country houses, bedroom arrangements were openly organized for the convenience of those who were currently enjoying a sexual liaison, regardless of marital status.

But the middle classes, now becoming prominent and ever conscious of the need to do the right thing, looked to Queen Victoria as their role model. She represented to them almost a mother figure, whose example must be followed, as though answering an unconscious need for the long-repressed Great Mother. The Queen herself is known to have thoroughly enjoyed her sexual relationship with her consort, Prince Albert, – what we think of as typically restrained Victorian behavior was most decidedly not a feature of the early years of her reign. However, after Prince Albert's death in 1861, the Queen went into unrelieved mourning. As a result, the behavior of a great number of her subjects changed and became extremely inhibited. When it became known that the Queen hated birth control, large families became the norm. However, because she loathed childbirth which she thought degrading, women took to wearing their corsets throughout pregnancy in order to preserve their dignity.

The Victorians took repression to even greater lengths than the Puritans in that sexual behavior was now restricted even within marriage. In part this was because of a popular theory of the time, reminiscent of Taoist belief, that semen was a vital substance and ejaculation a waste of it and to be avoided if possible. Sex was therefore to be limited to the minimum amount of activity needed for procreation. Avoidance of marital sex was also the result of the even more prevalent belief that men's sexual desires were bestial. As a result, a new myth began to grow up about women, at least those of a certain class. They were now considered to be pure, spiritual beings and therefore quite above sexuality. The ideal woman was required to be gentle and submissive, cherished and protected, and under no circumstances was she expected to enjoy so unrefined an activity as sexual intercourse. In his splendid book *The French Lieutenant's Woman*, subsequently made into a film, the author John Fowles explores in depth the effect of these attitudes on people of different temperaments.

The husband of high moral ideals aimed not only to impose himself as little as possible on his wife but also to refrain from sexual intercourse outside marriage. His wife, for her part, would endure his infrequent attentions without enthusiasm. The collective view of the proper demeanor for a wife during sex was that "a lady does not move." For a highly moral person, masturbation was considered particularly unacceptable. Not only did it not relate to procreation but it was generally thought that self-gratification could only lead to unseemly and unhealthy indulgence. Medical prejudice against masturbation had originated with the Swiss physician Tissot who, in the eighteenth century, taught that all sexual activity was dangerous. It caused blood to rush to the brain, the nerves became starved, and the likelihood of insanity therefore increased, a myth which was to have devastating consequences for many unfortunate souls.

Victorian investigators into sexuality, both in Europe and America, followed Tissot's lead in emphasising the dangers of sex and of masturbation in particular. As a background to this theory, they drew on the Biblical story Onan, who spilled his seed on the ground, thus avoiding

ONANIA:

OR, THE

HEINOUS SIN

OF

Self-Pollution,

AND ALL ITS

FRIGHTFUL CONSEQUENCES (in Both Sexes)

CONSIDERED:

With Spiritual and Physical ADVICE to those who have already injured themselves by this abominable Practice.

The EIGHTEENTH EDITION, as also the NINTH EDITION of the *SUPPLEMENT* to it, both of them Revised and Enlarged, and now Printed together in One Volume.

As the several Passages in the *Former* Impressions, that have been charged with being obscure and ambiguous, are, in these, cleared up and explained, there will be no more Alterations or Additions made.

And ONAN knew that the Seed should not be his: And it came to pass, when he went in unto his Brother's Wife, that he spilled it on the Ground, lest that he should give Seed to his Brother. And the Thing which he did, displeased the LORD; wherefore he slew him also. Gen. xxxviii. 9, 10.

Non Quis, Sed Quid.

LONDON:

Printed for H. COOKE, at the R Fleet-street, 1756.

[Price Bound . Shillings and Sixpence]

From the 18th century until recent times, the medical profession held some very curious views about the dangers of masturbation.

God's command to be fruitful and multiply. Physicians deduced from this that masturbation, since it was evidently a sin, would inevitably involve guilt. Thus it offered a convenient reason for mental illness, whose causes were otherwise largely unknown. In 1842, a doctor named Alfred Hitchcock urged his colleagues to be more vociferous in blaming illness on onanism. He claimed to have observed several fatal cases of over-indulgence in the practice.

Subsequently, medical writings increasingly linked insanity, illness and masturbation. In the mid-1800s attempts were sometimes made to cure insanity by castration. Although the subject was little discussed in relation to women, probably because such evidence of female interest in sex was thought too shocking, clitoridectomy was used as a cure for insanity. An alternative operation involved sewing together the vaginal lips so as to prevent access to the clitoris. Both doctors and priests were furthermore of the opinion that, by totally repressing the woman's sexuality, they would ensure her submissiveness to the man in her life.

A family gathering to celebrate the christening of Queen Victoria's daughter, Princess Victoria, the Princess Royal. Behind the respectable facade of Victorian family values lay a corrupt world involving mass child prostitution.

Close links were often made between "self-abuse" and homosexuality. In 1889, Joseph Howe stated that pederasts were diseased individuals whose problems originated in masturbatory activity which they had indulged in in youth. People feared that once a young man began to masturbate, he would lose interest in women, preferring to explore eroticism with those of his own sex. Adolescents were therefore given terrifying books to read that promised insanity and even an early grave as the consequence of solitary sexual activity. One Massachusetts physician warned young men that masturbation was the cause of inability to make what he called a "legitimate and permanent union with one of the other sex," probably a covert reference to homosexuality, which he dared not describe.

In America during the seventeenth and eighteenth centuries, almost any type of deviant behavior was classed as sodomy. Sermons and law cases indicate that the term applied equally to bestiality, mutual masturbation, and oral sex. Undaunted by the fact that they did not know exactly what it meant, Bible-belt Americans regarded sodomy as a sin. It became identified with evil to the extent that in the early days of Alabama, there was a town named Sodom. This in no way reflected the sexual activities of its inhabitants but was the result of their being regarded by neighboring towns as murderers and vandals. By the nineteenth century, the word "sodomy" had been replaced by the English phrase the "crime against nature," which many people understood even less.

Where homosexuality was concerned, the Victorians in England took a very hard line indeed. Until 1861, it carried the death sentence and was believed to incur eternal damnation. Even when this was no longer the case, a man could be imprisoned for life for his so-called "crime." Yet there is no doubt that the practice was widespread, particularly in the great English public schools. A journalist, William Stead, said at the time of the trial of Oscar Wilde, "...should everyone found guilty of Oscar Wilde's crime be imprisoned, there would be a very surprising emigration from Eton, Harrow, Rugby and Winchester to the jails of Pentonville and Holloway."

Prostitution

If the upright Victorian man was expected to inflict himself as little as possible on his wife and forbidden to masturbate, what was he to do? Clearly, few committed themselves to a state of semi-celibacy. Had they done so, there would not have been the vast number of prostitutes working in most European cities during this era. In London during the mid-nineteenth century, figures show that at least fifty thousand prostitutes were available, a large proportion of whom were no more than children who plied their trade under the guise of selling matches. Paris, Vienna and New York were also home to thousands of women who could find no other way of making a living. Many had originally been servants, seduced by a member of the family and then cast out as "fallen women," whose presence could not be allowed to sully the pure air of the house.

As in most societies throughout history, there was a world of difference between the lowly streetwalker and the courtesan who, as mistress of a rich and powerful man, would have an establishment provided for her.

Although not accepted into the highest levels of English society, these dashing ladies were nevertheless often the unacknowledged leaders of fashion. In Paris, always more openminded, matters were different. The demi-monde of the Second Empire was notable for the stylish women who were protected by rich aristocrats and businessmen. One of the best-known was Cora Pearl, mistress of more than one prince, who became a legend in her own time for extravagant gestures such as bathing in champagne in the presence of her dinner guests.

All cities had their quota of brothels, ranging from houses which rented out rooms by the hour to extremely luxurious establishments where the champagne flowed, the food was excellent and the girls the most accomplished. But at whichever end of the scale a man took his pleasure, the spectre of venereal disease was ever-present. Although the more professional women and those who worked from brothels tended to have regular medical examinations, there was no way of enforcing these upon the thousands of streetwalkers and others lower down the scale. Attempts to make medical examinations obligatory by law failed miserably. In any case, the treatment available for venereal disease was limited, mercury having some effect against syphilis but none at all in the case of gonorrhea. In America, concern about the health of the armed forces led to condoms being issued to sailors on leave and soldiers serving overseas during the First World War. This proved to be extremely effective.

Fear of venereal disease led to a demand for virgin prostitutes. One popular myth was that venereal disease might be cured by deflowering a young girl. As a result, some brothels employed doctors who would supply the customers with certificates attesting to a girl's virginity. As not even the most assiduous brothel-keeper could find a constant supply of virgins, the doctors also addressed themselves to ways in which virginity might be

The Sailors Adventure to the Streights of Merry-land or An Evening View on Ludgate Hill. Prostitutes and their prospective clients in 18th century London.

faked. The customer needed to be satisfied that the girl had bled after penetration, since this was considered indisputable proof of her virginal state. To this end, various ingenious methods were tried which involved inserting into the vagina various objects ranging from blood-soaked sponges to leeches.

The huge demand for child prostitutes was but one of many symptoms of the sickness of Victorian society. Outwardly respectable to the point of stultification, the underlying shadow encompassed extremes of vice. Women suffered particularly since the moral code of the age required them to be either angels or whores, echoes of which continued to reverberate well into the twentieth century.

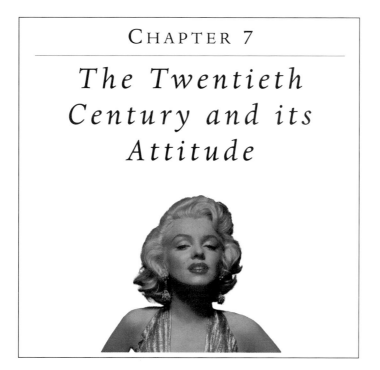

CHAPTER 7

The Twentieth Century and its Attitude

W E HAVE ARRIVED in the twentieth century. What has been the nature of sexual mythology in this era? Two overriding themes predominate: sex as the object of scientific and psychological investigation and sex as a commodity to be exploited on the grand scale.

The Scientific Approach

For the last hundred years and more, we have looked to science to provide the answers we seek about what makes life as it is. Sexuality has not escaped the modern microscope. In 1948 and 1953, Alfred Kinsey published the results of more than eighteen thousand personal interviews about people's sexual behavior. Although he took every possible precaution to ensure that his subjects were not lying, many people simply could not believe that his results were legitimate. Some felt that even this number of interviews could not do justice to the full spectrum of human sexual behavior. This probably indicates a refusal to believe that Americans could

OPPOSITE: Darcey Bussell, Belinda Hatley and Jonathan Cope, stars of the Royal Ballet, Covent Garden, London, perform *Dances with Death*, a modern ballet about AIDS.

be engaging in so many sexual activities, which were, according to the official stance on morality, unnatural. People were shocked to discover the high level of infidelity within marriage and the fact that some seventy percent of the male population had visited a prostitute. Even more outrageous was the finding that a considerable proportion of people had experienced homosexual relationships. Many Americans preferred to subscribe to the myth of the happy, stable, nuclear family as the norm.

Dr Alfred Kinsey, the American whose researches into sexual behavior were the subject of emormous controversy.

From this time on, the sexologists began to come into their own. In 1966, Masters and Johnson published their research into the physiology of orgasm. With the cooperation of volunteers who were prepared to engage in coitus in the presence of both investigators and technicians, they measured vaginal responses using a penis-like object made of clear plastic, enabling them to film inside the vagina. Sex, hitherto considered basically a private matter, at least in Western culture, had now gone public. Although Masters and Johnson in many ways demythologized sex, they also created a new type of myth, namely that sexual response can be measured in solely physical terms and meaningful conclusions drawn from the results. If sex is anything more than physical coupling, such research can yield only partial truths. Nevertheless, Masters and Johnson were instrumental in overturning the Victorian idea that the focus of a woman's sexual activity was primarily on servicing the male. Their findings indicated conclusively that women have a greater capacity for orgasm than men, a fact which had, incidentally, been known to the Taoists for hundreds of years.

On a lighter note, sex manuals, which had until this time focused on the mechanics of intercourse, now emphasized ways to maximize pleasure. With their clear and sensual drawings, manuals such as *The Joy of Sex* bore a more than passing resemblance to their Oriental counterparts.

Birth Control and Abortion

The scientific approach to sex during the twentieth century has resulted in a dramatic change in attitudes toward contraception. Throughout history, few topics have been so bound up in myth, taboo, and superstition. It is equally true that few topics have been the cause of such strong feelings which, during the current century, have polarized forces into the patriarchal at one end of the spectrum and the feminist at the other. The former, which numbers a surprising number of women among its supporters, takes the view that God's plan must under no circumstances be interfered with. No matter what the cost to the mother, the possibility of conception may not be avoided nor a pregnancy interfered with. This is a belief-system based on the idea of predestination, current for centuries and firmly upheld in the Western World by the Roman Catholic Church. But it harks back also to the punitive figure of Jehovah who decreed that women must suffer to atone for Eve's disobedience.

The feminist view is that a woman's body is her own and she is therefore entitled to have a choice in terms of what happens to it. Quality of life, always a feminine concern, is also an issue here, as opposed to quantity, required by the commandment to "go forth and multiply." From the feminist standpoint, abortion is not a transgression against divine law. What it does offend is patriarchal prejudice, and it is this which causes so many women to feel guilty about their decision to terminate a pregnancy.

Until the advent of modern contraceptive methods, people had for hundreds of years been trying to find a foolproof way of avoiding conception, whether it be *coitus interruptus* or a sponge placed in the vagina to block the entrance to the womb, or various primitive types of condoms, made of substances like sheep gut or fish skin. Given the size of a great many families, these methods obviously had only limited success.

Around the beginning of this century, among the poor where families of sixteen were not unknown, there was untold misery. Appalling housing conditions, malnutrition, constant childbearing, and the loss of children through childhood disease was the lot of the nineteenth-century, working-class woman. Many, in despair, resorted to primitive methods of do-it-yourself abortion, usually by introducing a foreign object such as a knitting needle into the womb. Horrific injuries and death could and often did ensue. For a single woman of any class, of course, pregnancy constituted a great disgrace. It often meant that she was thrown out of her home and left to fend for herself as best she could, which usually meant prostitution.

In England, birth control for the masses was pioneered by Marie Stopes. Born in 1880 into an academic family, she was a strong-minded and intellectually brilliant woman. While still a virgin she wrote *Married Love*, which explained the mechanics of sex. The book encouraged readers to throw off the inhibitions of the usual Victorian upbringing and fully enjoy their sexual relationships. Outrageous in its time, the book became an enormous bestseller throughout the world. As a result, Stopes received countless letters from married couples who appreciated her views and hoped that she might also be able to advise them on contraception. She duly obliged with *Wise Parenthood*, which offered detailed advice on the various contraceptive methods available, from caps to the so-called "safe" period for intercourse. In 1921, Marie Stopes opened a birth control clinic in London in the face of massive opposition from both the Catholic church and the medical profession, which regarded control of feminine sexuality as the province of men only. Although she was not so radical as to allow the clinic to care for the unmarried, it proved an untold blessing to thousands of women.

Marie Stopes's motives were, however, not entirely altruistic. She had developed an interest in the science of eugenics, to which she became passionately committed. This highly elitist doctrine was based on the myth that the perfectly fit and healthy specimen of humanity was the only acceptable one. Contraception was, in her view, primarily a way of ensuring that women from poorer economic groups, who were therefore more likely to produce unhealthy offspring, had fewer of them.

Stopes's views on eugenics were shared by the

Marie Stopes, 1880-1958, who championed the cause of birth control and thereby transformed the lives of countless women.

leader of the birth control movement in America, Margaret Sanger. She had gained wide experience as an obstetric nurse working with underprivileged families and single mothers. Incensed by the high mortality rate for both mothers and babies, and especially by the damage caused by self-induced abortion, Sanger decided that women must be liberated from unwanted pregnancies. In 1914, she started a magazine initially called *The Woman Rebel* and later known as the *Birth Control Review*. She went on in 1921 to found the American Birth Control League. Her heroic efforts were rewarded when doctors were finally allowed to prescribe contraceptives.

Sex and the Psyche

Few intellectual movements in history have had an impact on Western attitudes comparable to that of psychoanalysis, particularly in the area of sexuality. Sigmund Freud, the father of psychoanalysis, proposed concepts which have become a form of new mythology, profoundly influencing collective attitudes toward sex. At a time of great repressiveness, Freud's work between 1900-10, was revolutionary in bringing sexuality into a more conscious realm. Nonetheless, he was a Victorian man and this is very much reflected in his thinking. According to his scheme of things, women were inherently limited, which meant that feminine values were inevitably considered inferior. Two of Freud's most basic hypotheses are the castration complex and penis envy, both of which rest on the assumption that the female genitalia are, somehow, lacking in relation to the male.

Freud's greatest value for the twentieth century was that he brought to collective attention the reality of the "unconscious." He pointed out that much of what happens to an individual during his or her lifetime can be interpreted in terms of unconscious symbolism. Where he fell short, however, was in his conviction that such symbolism is based exclusively on sexuality. As we shall see, Jung was to point out the limitations of this view. Sex, according to Freud, is the underlying force which drives our lives, determining our attitudes and conduct. His model for the emotional development of children involved identifying different stages of the growth of sexuality from infanthood onwards, a most revolutionary idea at that time. Neurosis, he believed, was the result of one of these stages not having been successfully completed, which then gave rise to sexual repression of one kind or another.

Essentially patriarchal, Freud's thinking can be traced back to the influence of the story of Adam and Eve in which Eve is created out of Adam's rib. In other words, woman is somehow inferior to man: he is complete but she is essentially lacking. As we know, this myth underlies the Judeo-Christian and Muslim traditions in ways that affect almost every aspect of life. Freud takes up this message yet again, this time in psychological guise. He believed that once a little girl has seen her brother's penis and compared it with her own genitals, she automatically thinks that hers must be lacking something. Freud then concludes that this moment of realization is the beginning of a lifelong process for the girl, declaring that "...her whole development may be said to take place under the colors of envy for the penis." The lack of a phallus, he believed, so disadvantages women that it makes them more masochistic and narcissistic than men, lacking the moral fiber, which, for some reason best known to himself, he believed distinguishes the male of the species. Aristotle, with his view of women as "deficient males," could not have done better.

While Freud's hypothetical little girl is beginning to be aware of her natural inferiority, her young brother experiences something entirely different when he first notices that her genitalia are quite unlike his own. Because he thinks that to have a penis is the normal state, he assumes, according to Freud, that she has been castrated. "Probably no male human being is spared the terrifying shock of threatened castration at the sight of the female genitals," states Freud. This trauma sets in motion a fear of feminine sexuality. Jung was later of the opinion that these views reflected Freud's own experience rather than a general truth.

Puberty was another area to occupy Freud's attention. During puberty, boys, he thought, experience a surge in libido or sexual energy. A girl, on the other hand, undergoes the opposite, a kind of wave of repression of sexuality. As a child, her libido had focused on her clitoris, a version of the penis, although naturally much inferior – Freud described it as "masculine machinery." By the time she is a mature woman, her clitoral sexuality has faded away. Now it is the turn of her vaginal cavity, understood as the opposite of the penis, to be erotically charged and therefore the place where orgasm is experienced. In order to understand how a girl turns into a woman, said Freud, "we must follow the further vicissitudes of the excitability of the clitoris." In 1905, he declared that all adult women should expect vaginal orgasm as the norm. This was a new departure since until then the only form of female orgasm was thought to be clitoral. The controversy about vaginal versus clitoral orgasm continues to this day.

Because women are by nature inferior, in Freud's view, it follows that fatherhood is a state far superior to motherhood. In this, Freud was again subject to the influence of an age-old belief, based on Roman law, according to which paternity was thought to be a matter of opinion and will. Nobody, after all, could ever be absolutely certain about the identity of a child's father. Later, the Church authorities argued that whereas motherhood is self-evident from the senses alone, fatherhood was a supposition based on an inference and therefore must be a superior state. Freud's version was that fatherhood represents a victory of the elevated and refined intellect over the gross and sensual.

Freud looked directly to Greek mythology to describe that stage of childhood sexuality he called the Oedipus complex. From the very beginning, he believed, infants are sexual beings. At a very young age, possibly as early as two, this generalized sexuality is focused on a specific object. In practice, this means that the small child develops an erotic attachment to the parent of the opposite sex along with feelings of aggressive rivalry to the same-sex parent. In due course, fear of punishment makes the child give up these feelings, and identify with the same-sex parent in the hope of one day acquiring a sexual partner of his or her own. This idea, scandalous in its time, was based on the story of the mythical king Oedipus who killed his father and married his mother. In fact, Freud seems to have been unaware that the myth related to the normal archaic custom whereby the queen took as her consort a younger lover who had then to kill the old king.

In devaluing the feminine and ascribing a superior value to the role of father, Freud paid insufficient attention to the importance of the early bonding of mother and child. The neuroses he ascribes to repressed sexuality are more often the result of a failure to bond, a psychological fact rooted in the mythology of the Great Mother. Carl Gustav Jung, the Swiss psychiatrist who was originally a student of Freud, was later to point out that different patterns of parent-child relationship can be described by a wide range of myths, not just the Oedipal. He rejected what he perceived as Freud's inclination to build a psychological system on his own personal experience and then apply it universally.

Although Jung was, at the beginning of his professional life, an adherent of Freudian psychology, he broke with Freud in 1913. The basis of the split was Jung's proposal that libido comprised not only sexual energy but psychic energy as a whole. He had arrived at this understanding from his study of the fantasies of a woman in the early stages of schizophrenia. The images she described repeated themes from myths which were thousands of years old and which she had never read. Since the images could not possibly be interpreted in terms of repressed sexuality, Jung concluded that Freud's theory was inadequate. What Freud called the unconscious was now referred to by Jung as the "personal unconscious," the home of those aspects of ourselves which we repress. Underlying this, however, is the "collective unconscious," comprising all human knowledge and experience, a kind of unconscious Internet.

After his break with Freud, Jung experienced a long and difficult period of introspection. His explorations of the far shores of the inner world afforded him insights of breathtaking importance. To this day, we have hardly begun to understand the ramifications for the human condition of his discoveries. In attempting to understand myths in psychological terms, Jung realized that they are vehicles of information about the archetypal forces of the collective unconscious which shape our lives for better or worse. He was in fact responsible for bringing into popular usage the term "archetype," meaning, as we saw in chapter 1, an inbuilt pattern of human behavior common to all people, everywhere, for example: father, mother, money, power. In this he was totally at odds with Freud, whose view was that our actions are primarily dominated by our sexual drive. Jung's thinking about sexuality was in terms of the archetypes of the masculine and feminine and the way in which they relate to each other.

According to Jung the prince and princess of the fairy tale who live happily ever after represent the feminine and masculine components of the psyche. Every man carries within him an image of the ideal feminine. Similarly, every woman has her inborn image of man. The man's inner and therefore unconscious feminine side Jung called the "anima," from the Latin word for soul. To the masculine aspect of a woman's unconscious he gave the name "animus," meaning mind or spirit. To harmonize masculine and feminine is to make the inner marriage whereby a human being finally becomes a whole person. This is a development of the ancient theme of the sacred marriage, which Jung further investigated in his extensive study of alchemy. In alchemical medieval texts, the marriage of the two opposing energies is represented by pictures of the King and Queen locked in a sexual embrace.

In studying the psychology of relationships, Jung observed that what happens when we fall in love is that we project our inner contra-sexual image onto a member of the opposite sex. This image may bear little relationship to what the person receiving the projection is actually like. Young people, and sometimes the not-so young also, often do this first with somebody they do not personally know, usually a celebrity such as a sports hero or a rock star. Literary figures such as Heathcliff and Mr. Darcy fulfill a similar function, as did the original superstar, Lord Byron. It is a safe way of taking the first steps along the road of Eros since the chances of ever actually meeting the object of passion are minimal. Were that to happen, the starstruck youngster would probably be struck dumb, totally unable to relate to the hero or heroine as another person.

Sooner or later, the projection of animus or anima is focused onto somebody one actually does know and the process we call "falling in love" is set in motion. As partners begin to get to know each other better, the projections begin to dissolve. It becomes clear that the object of one's love is not a Prince Charming or the Ideal Woman but a human being like oneself. At this stage, many relationships flounder, one or both parties having fallen out of love. Yet it is exactly at this point that the hard work of real love can in fact begin. Jung understood marriage as a psychological relationship which provides the couple with the opportunity to realize the fullness of their own individual development. But this requires patience, commitment and a great deal of faith.

Jung's thinking was just as revolutionary as

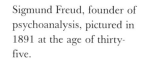

Sigmund Freud, founder of psychoanalysis, pictured in 1891 at the age of thirty-five.

Freud's had been earlier. In an era and a culture where woman was seen as the weaker vessel, Jung insisted that in order for a man to become whole, he must consciously incorporate his feminine qualities, the opposite being true for a woman. He is often criticized for his definitions of masculine and feminine since they are almost inevitably colored by the accepted ideas of his day. Yet this does not detract from the fact that Jung was a great and influential supporter of the values of the feeling and intuitive side of life. This is no mean feat when we consider that, for the last two thousand years or more, these had been largely dismissed as irrational and therefore trivial in comparison with the all-important, traditionally masculine, attributes of reason and the intellect.

In the field of anthropology discoveries have also been made that have opened Western eyes to the appallingly inadequate nature of many of our beliefs about sexuality. An outstanding contribution in this area was made by the anthropologist Margaret Mead. She explored the social structures and sexual mores of tribal societies, living for long periods within the communities she was studying. Her findings gave the Western world an entirely new perspective on sexual behavior. Women were not treated by all societies everywhere as inferior. Mead demonstrated that what is taken for granted as the norm in one society may be wholly unacceptable to another which subscribes to entirely different myths. She drew to public attention the fact that premarital sex, considered by Western culture at that time as beyond the pale, was absolutely the norm in societies such as Polynesia.

Feminism

In 1950 the Catholic Church formally proclaimed the Assumption of the Virgin Mary into heaven. Jung considered this to be a most important development for the collective psyche. He pointed out that the Assumption of the Virgin featured neither in scripture nor in early Christian tradition. Yet it gradually developed as a collective opinion so powerful that it was finally condoned as official dogma by the Pope, despite the lack of scriptural proof. For Jung, Mary provided the fourth, feminine element missing from the Trinity of Father, Son and Holy Ghost, and marked a definite movement away from the patriachal society. His views were vindicated within a relatively short space of time, when the voice of the feminist movement began to be heard.

From the late 1960s the development of the contraceptive Pill had an incalculable effect on women. Many felt that it represented their greatest step towards freedom since the acquisition of the vote. Enabled to engage in sex without fear of pregnancy, women inevitably began to question the old sexual belief-systems. Feminist writers like Germaine Greer and others took issue with the collective attitudes to women. In her book *The Female Eunuch*, published in 1970, Greer unmasked and attacked the stereotypical roles to which women had been subjected for centuries. She debunked the myth of the masterful male and the passive female who depends on him totally for her well-being. The reaction had begun against thousands of years of patriarchal rule. Women were no longer to be seen as playthings or domestic slaves.

Germaine Greer, Australian writer and feminist, who rose to fame with her book *The Female Eunuch*.

Yet in retrospect, they still had a long way to travel towards the goal of taking charge of their own lives. Young women freed from the fear of unwanted pregnancy often became enslaved to the expectation that they would automatically be willing to have sex. Patriarchal attitudes die hard and many a girl, unsure of herself and desperately anxious to please and be thought "cool," consented to a sexual relationship she did not really want which often resulted in a mindless promiscuity. Happily, matters began to change for the better during the eighties and nineties, not least because of the fear of AIDS. More emphasis was put on the quality of relationships, and excessive promiscuity was no longer seen as admirable. Some even considered it an addiction, and clinics began to offer appropriate treatment. That there could be such a thing as "free love" was one of the biggest myths of all. There is always a price to be paid.

Carrying the image of the virgin during the Easter Festival, Algarve, Portugal.

The Gay Liberation Movement

Some people have felt that the price paid for practicing homosexuality is AIDS. The century has witnessed major changes in attitudes toward homosexuality. At the end of the last millennium, Oscar Wilde was consigned to Reading Gaol for committing "the sin that dare not speak its name." Nowadays, all large cities in the West have areas almost exclusively devoted to gay culture, bars, restaurants, and shops. The gay cause has been championed by filmmakers like Derek Jarman, artists, of whom David Hockney is a notable example, and many others, including the colorful and eccentric Quentin Crisp. This is particularly challenging for bastions of patriarchal values like the Church and, in particular, the armed forces.

The gay community has been held largely to blame for the rapid rise of AIDS. A recent opinion poll showed that a third of the population of the UK believe that AIDS is a punishment for moral laxity, essentially meaning homosexuality. That it can be transmitted heterosexually and also as a result of infected blood from donors seems to have been largely overlooked. From a mythological point of view, it is interesting that the disease is transmitted via blood and semen. We have seen in earlier chapters how these substances have, throughout history, been considered as mystical transmitters of the life force. And the illness does, of course, involve the progressive breakdown of the immune system, so the life force slowly, inexorably and inevitably weakens. Although AIDS has given rise to a major campaign to practice "safe sex," many, and young people in particular, continue to believe that it is something "which could never happen to me."

Quentin Crisp, eccentric Englishman said to have once described himself as "One of England's stately homos."

Sex, Drugs, and Rock 'n Roll – and the Silver Screen

Greta Garbo, a goddess of the silver screen, seen here with Robert Taylor in *Camille,* 1937. She retired at the height of her popularity and became a recluse.

With the revolution in sexual behavior during the sixties, the repressed energy of years surfaced with a vengeance. Young people on both sides of the Atlantic rebelled against their parents' values and lifestyles, which they saw as inhibited and boring. Sexually permissive, the young began to experiment with drugs and, above all, to listen to music. With the advent of the Beatles, the mythology of the rock star as god was born. Other groups quickly followed. Mick Jagger strutted and pranced, the adoring girls screamed, it was as though the spirit of Dionysus had been evoked. As indeed it had – deep within the collective unconscious of the music-lovers. Yet the songs of these modern troubadours could also be extremely patriarchal: Jagger boasted of having his girl under his thumb and girls in general were referred to in many songs as "baby." A blatant form of phallus-worship was practiced by certain groupies who followed the rock stars in their royal progress around the world, offering their sexual services. As a memento of the occasion, they would make a plaster cast of the penis of whichever luminary they had entertained.

It is not only in the world of music that we have created contemporary gods and goddesses. As we know, the divinities of ancient cultures personified the qualities valued at that time. In Greece they lived on Mount Olympus. During this century, they have tended to live in Hollywood, sexually charismatic men and women who enact the rites of love for us on screen. Where Aphrodite and Venus represented the ideal of love, beauty and sexuality, the twentieth century has given this role to Marilyn Monroe, Greta Garbo, Julia Roberts, and Madonna, to name but a few. The gods have been embodied in men like Rudolph Valentino, Erroll Flynn, Clark Gable, Robert Redford and Richard Gere. In ancient times, devotees brought valuable offerings to the shrine of the gods they favored. Today we take our money to the box office.

Representations of sexuality have changed quite dramatically since the early years of motion pictures. At first, cinema focused on the romantic myth of boy meeting girl, falling in love, enduring some pain, but living happily ever after. That this is essentially what people want is proved by the fact that romantic films far outnumber every other kind. Hollywood told fairy tales of handsome heroes rescuing beautiful damsels in distress. As censorship gradually relaxed, sex scenes became ever more explicit. Now it is taken for granted that sex sells films. It has become a commodity both in terms of the big screen and, much more perniciously, in the world of advertising, which uses both film and magazines to convey its messages. As a result, we are constantly bombarded with sexual images whose message is that happiness and fulfillment depend on being young, beautiful and seductive. This is a myth that belongs entirely in the patriarchal tradition. Permissive we may be, but in terms of personal freedom we have still a long way to go.

Marilyn Monroe, who carried the archetype of the goddess of Love, a burden too great for any human being to bear. She could not overcome her image of a brainless sex-symbol and died in tragic circumstances.

CHAPTER 8

What Lies Ahead?

W E ARE APPROACHING THE END of a century which has seen more change than at any other period in history. In the Western world, in particular, attitudes toward sexuality are in the midst of a radical upheaval. How can we, as men and women, go forward in a creative and optimistic way? Will the old myths serve as an adequate basis on which to build, or do we need to create new ones? Perhaps by looking at current trends and their significance, we can understand how matters might develop and what could be done in order to help that process unfold in an intelligent way.

At this time, it seems to me that the opposing forces of patriarchal and feminist attitudes are beginning to polarize in an extreme, and therefore disturbing, way. But there is much we can do to help create a healthier balance of the two. Jung constantly emphasized the overriding importance of becoming more conscious. But people today are deeply hypnotized by the concept of the expert, one of the greatest myths of all, and a regression to the need for a parent who will tell us what to do. We look to experts to comment on every facet of life and provide us with the ideal solution to

OPPOSITE: Hippies, travelers and popular music fans of all ages gather at the annual Glastonbury festival, England.

whatever the problem may be. Nowhere is this more so than in the field of sexuality. The expert is only too ready to tell us how to attract a partner, how to improve our relationships, how to give birth. Until we are prepared to listen to our own instincts and trust our own judgment, we cannot hope to become more conscious.

At present we are, on the one hand, seeing an increasing interest both in fundamental Christianity and in Islam. In both of these we are at the extreme patriarchal end of the spectrum, where masculine values rule without question. What is particularly interesting is the growing support for these religious systems among women. Only recently *The Times* in London reported that Muslim women in Kenya threatened to boycott the new national identity cards unless they were allowed to wear their veils for the required photographs. In the UK women are converting to Islam in noticeable numbers. When interviewed about their reasons for taking what would appear to be a step backward, they claim to feel protected and more feminine behind their veils. Not only do they believe that men respect them more but they also have a greater sense of security. In other words, they know their place just as women have been obliged to do for the last two thousand years and more. The myth of Big Daddy who controls the woman, the weaker vessel, and knows what is best for her, is still well and truly alive.

At the other end of the spectrum, we have the more extreme results of the feminist movement, whereby a woman prefers to take total responsibility for herself in all areas of life, with no recourse whatsoever to a man. More and more women are bringing up their families alone. Many, of course, do so out of necessity, but for others it is a conscious choice and one which is increasingly possible in these days of sperm banks and in-vitro fertilization. An actual male partner is no longer necessary for the woman who wants motherhood. Other women have children by several different fathers who may or may not subsequently play a role in the development of their offspring. Here are echoes of the earliest times when paternity was neither known nor much cared about, predicated upon the myth of the goddess with her child. But human women are not goddesses any more than men are gods. Given good mothering, girls may not suffer too much from the lack of a father. But for a boy it is a different matter. The old myths tell us how the son of the goddess eventually became her lover and herein lies the danger.

Far too many boys are growing up without a male role model. To understand the significance of this phenomenon and where it might lead, we can look to Jung's description of the archetype of the father. In all mythologies, the father stands in the role of authority, lawgiver, carrier of the structures and values that support life. Because the human psyche is pre-programmed with this archetype, even the gentlest father will represent authority to his young children and will carry it for them until they have developed a sense of their own inner authority. If the father fails to perform his archetypal role, or the single mother does not discipline as well as nurture, the son will remain a boy. However, in a tribal society, he would be uninitiated, an outcast from the community, unable to take up his responsibilities as a man.

What is the exception among native peoples is rapidly becoming the norm in our own culture. Yet we can take heart from the fact that boys often unconsciously attempt to find solutions for themselves. They create gangs, often with their own initiation rituals, involving physical ordeals of some kind. The problem is that these "tribes" often move about on the edge of society, experiencing themselves as outlaws. They remain strangers to the sense of dignity and self-respect that comes from knowing one is making a valuable and valued contribution to the community. Their preferred style of behavior is usually of an extremely macho variety, so they are unable to have satisfactory relationships with women. This is not to be wondered at since they are unconsciously trying to separate themselves from the world of the mother. If we are to create a healthier culture, we must find a way of providing

Figure of a Sleeping Hermaphrodite.
Greece, 2nd century BC. The hermaphrodite which exhibits both male and female sexual chracteristics, represents the inner contrasexual element within us all.

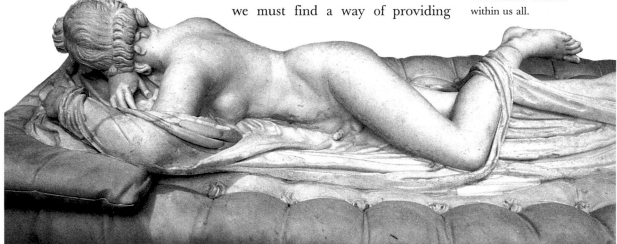

boys with a contemporary rite of passage that will enable them to find their identity as men.

What form could this take? Conscription, or the draft, is the oft-quoted way. Yet we cannot turn the clock back and military service is anyway based on the patriarchal myth of the conquering hunter-killer. Although perhaps necessary in countries which live under threat of invasion, it will not serve to create a different vision for the future. More to the point would be community service or team projects which would require boys to take responsibility for the well-being of others. Such an initiation would help them to develop both self-discipline and compassion. It would also serve the purpose of making the young man fit for marriage. Many a young woman nowadays sees no future for herself as the wife of an unstable boy. She would rather use him to father the child she wants and then continue on alone, which, unfortunately, only serves to perpetuate the cycle.

In other parts of society, notably among the middle classes, many men are involving themselves in the "New Age" movement with its emphasis on the traditionally feminine realm of feelings and relatedness. They are beginning to explore the more tender and vulnerable aspect of their nature and, as a result, their relationships with their womenfolk and children. Yet this process, worthwhile and necessary in itself, is not proving totally satisfactory. Women complain that their men are becoming almost too gentle and caring, to the detriment of their essential masculine sexuality. It is no wonder that many men are feeling confused about their identity and resentful about the differing expectations women have of them. What is the way ahead here?

In the United States, the poet Robert Bly has begun a movement based on the ideas in his book *Iron John*. This is essentially a story about a boy's initiation process. He must cut the ties that hold him to his mother and make a relationship with the deep masculine aspect of his psyche, which Bly refers to as "the wild man." Bly's work has become the object of satire in many quarters, which only serves to demonstrate the fear of losing the status quo experienced by many men and the deep suspicion with which they regard inner work. I would propose that workshops of this kind become a normal part of the educational curriculum. Girls would benefit from similar instruction while older children could explore these issues in mixed groups. All children should be introduced to mythology at an early stage and helped to understand how the myths pertaining to sexuality in its widest sense have created the society in which we live. Such a curriculum would also incorporate the needs of those who by nature are inclined to homosexuality and ensure that they are not marginalized. If we want to create a more intelligent structure for ourselves, we had better begin at the beginning, with children and what they are taught. Children taught to value themselves and others could transform society within a generation or two.

Girls also need initiation procedures to meet their own needs, which are

The Androgyne, born of the union between Mercury and Venus, from the 1618 edition of Michael Maier's *Atalanta Fugiens*.

quite different. The majority of girls, even today, have no trouble at all putting the feelings of others before their own, especially the feelings of male others. Initiation for a girl needs to be an educational process whereby she studies the way in which the patriarchy has operated for the last few thousand years and how this affects her own life today. For a woman, the process of self-realization almost always involves a process of waking up from her deeply programmed automatic behavior. But this is something which many women do not undertake until around mid-life, by which time they have often brought up daughters and perpetuated the process. Girls need to discover how to support feminine values before they embark upon relationships and childbearing, enabling them to resist coercion and exercise choice. They must be able to question just how far they want to adopt the patriarchal way of life, with its emphasis on status and achievement. Many an outwardly liberated woman of today finds herself in the position of trying to juggle the roles of wife, mother and career-woman and to do them all well. Exhaustion, feelings of inadequacy and subliminal guilt are too often the result.

One result of the current confusion about sexual identity is the popularity of the androgynous figure, especially in the world of fashion. For many young people, the dictates of fashion play a major role in their lives. At an age when it is desperately important to be approved of by one's peers, the currently acceptable image is the androgynous one. Unfortunately, the nature of the myth of the androgyne is not generally understood, with unhappy consequences. The word "androgyne" derives from the combination of Greek words for man and woman. It is therefore an autonomous being, half male and half female, and as a symbol it is found in many cultures, from ancient Mesopotamia to the Indo-Europeans and the indigenous peoples of Africa, Australia and North America. In the Upanishads, for instance, Prajapati, the Lord of creatures, is described as an androgyne. Alone and lonely, he makes himself fall into two halves which then become husband and wife, whose subsequent copulation produces human beings. Other members of the Indian pantheon, Siva and Parvati, are sometimes represented as an androgyne, symbolizing the state of completeness arising from inner union.

Psychologically speaking, androgyny is about relating to the contra-sexual element within ourselves, not identifying with it. It is not so much a case of a woman being more like a man as of relating to her own inner

Brides of Christ become performing artists. *The Singing Nuns*, a group from the London-based Catholic Order of Sion, seen here during a concert they gave in 1966.

masculine energy, which helps her to discriminate and discern what is good for her. But this is not what fashion encourages. The trend towards boyish, super-thin fashion models, of which Twiggy was a forerunner in the sixties, now produces young women like Kate Moss, who is doubtless naturally extremely thin. Unfortunately, many girls and young women who are not, have adopted her as a role model, starving themselves in their efforts to emulate her. Often the end result is an eating disorder, anorexia or bulimia.

Anorexia nervosa produces a body image which denies all manifestations of sexuality. Although the causes of this life-threatening disease are complex, especially since young men can also be affected, there is no doubt that the fashion industry has a great deal to answer for. Rather than being encouraged to be proud of their burgeoning sexuality, many girls are slavishly attempting to eradicate any sign of it. The multi-million-dollar diet industry also takes advantage of the current collective fear of the flesh. Many anorexics are also punishing a mother who failed to meet their emotional needs. Reluctance to take food into oneself is, on one level, a statement about being unwilling to engage with life itself, to trust the natural processes that are the domain of the Great Mother. What else do we see here if not the result of patriarchal prejudice against the body in favor of the spirit?

There is no easy answer because what is involved is the need for a reconnection with the feminine divine principle. This, in turn, would mean a proper recognition of the inestimable value of motherhood, a role which the patriarchy takes completely for granted. Yet it is perfectly happy to pay corporate executives vast salaries to promote products nobody actually needs. Since our culture shows its appreciation of value through the medium of money, mothers will need to be paid. This would put their value in line with that of nannies, at the very least.

Another rite of passage which is in a state of transition is marriage. As we have seen, in the earliest agricultural civilizations, the sacred marriage between the virgin Mother-goddess and her son-lover, between priestess and king, was thought essential to the continuing fertility of the land. In temples, the rite was carried out by priest and priestess in a specifically sexual way. During the Middle Ages the roles were reversed. Now the rite took the form of an inner, subjective phenomenon, whereby the human soul, understood as female, married Christ, the divine male. Nuns to this day are called "brides of Christ." The myth of the sacred marriage is one of the most ancient and most powerful of all and is still very much alive, judging by the enormous interest shown throughout the world in a royal marriage. Yet recent royal marriages, at any rate in the UK, have collapsed in spectacular fashion. This is perhaps just one of the signs that we need to reevaluate our marriage myths.

In Western society the myth of the soul mate dies hard. We have the romantic yearning for the other, the lost half of ourselves, as Plato thought, who will complete us. Like the prince and the princess of fairy-tales, we hope then to live happily ever after. That the books of romance writer Barbara Cartland sell in their millions the world over attests to this fact. But marriage was never intended to be a lifelong love affair, something which was much better understood by the adherents

Kate Moss, a model whose waif-like proportions have influenced the perception of what constitutes a desirable body-image for many young girls.

of courtly love in medieval France than by Western people at the end of the twentieth century. Today we do not, on the whole, marry for dynastic reasons so we marry for love. Or at least what we believe to be love, which is often, alas, no more than a rosy glow of sexual excitement combined with a high degree of projection and romantic illusion. Commitment to the relationship, a feeling of responsibility for someone else's well-being, the ability to accept and forgive sound dull by comparison.

In some cultures, such as India, the marriage ceremony continues for three days, at the end of which the couple undoubtedly feel married, conscious of having undergone a rite of passage. Things are very different in the West. Here a marriage can happen more or less on a whim, what passes for a ceremony taking only a few minutes to complete. Those who want something more substantial might spend vast amounts of money on a lavish wedding. But the significance of a true rite of passage is that the outer event becomes incorporated into the psyche as an inner reality. Only then can it change the person. No amount of money can cause that to happen.

So deeply entrenched in the collective psyche is the idea of marriage that, in spite of the fact that about one in two marriages in the USA end in divorce and one in three marriages in the UK, people still keep searching for the right mate. But serial monogamy is an unsatisfactory answer for many reasons, not least the welfare of children who have no extended family as a constant source of emotional support. Perhaps we could learn something from the French. The funeral of President Mitterand of France was attended both by his wife and his long-standing mistress, Anne Pingeot, who was present with her daughter by the President.

It is hard to imagine many countries where such an event would be collectively sanctioned. Yet in the wealthier French families, there is a long tradition of the husband keeping a mistress while his wife has a lover. Formal divorce is difficult in France, for it not only has a strong Catholic tradition, but also a system of inheritance and marital laws which are tied to property. The French, ever pragmatic, have accepted that romance is one thing and marriage, at least in the longer term, another. Yet they see no reason why both cannot be incorporated into a life. There is no stigma attached to the role of mistress, and friends and associates, when issuing invitations, will discreetly inquire as to which partner will attend.

Such an arrangement may not suit everybody. Yet the current high rate of marital breakdown in countries where divorce is easier does not make for a well-balanced society. Both emotionally and economically, the effect is often disastrous. What then is the solution? Some people, especially in the UK, think that the problem can be solved by making divorce harder. Certainly it is essential that people should be required to make an effort to work out their difficulties. Yet how many have the resources they need to do so? The time to start is before the marriage has taken place. A period of preparation should be compulsory during which the couple can explore exactly what they expect from their union and what they are willing to put into it. Since marriage, like parenthood, is one of the most important experiences most people will have during their lifetime, it seems curious that so many people are prepared for neither.

Any relationship is likely to work better where the people concerned are prepared to take responsibility for themselves and their own behavior. Nowhere is this more so than in marriage. Rather than expecting our partner to meet all our needs, blaming them when they fail to do so, we must be prepared to look much more to our own resources to find the fulfillment we seek. As we have seen, Jung has a great deal to teach us about finding within ourselves those qualities we attribute to another. The myths for the twenty-first century need to incorporate respect for the values of both masculine and feminine.

Sex education as it is presently practiced in most schools is extremely inadequate. It is all well and good to teach children about the mechanics of procreation, and of course they must be informed about contraception and the risk of venereal disease and AIDS. But this is to teach only the science of sex and ignore the fact that it is also an art and a fundamental human experience. Central to all such teaching needs to be the issue of relationship which, of necessity, includes a proper study of psychology. Young people need to learn that sex is not about the use and abuse of power. Recent figures in the USA show that more than a third of girls under sixteen have had a sexual relationship. By the time they are eighteen, almost a quarter of eighteen-year-old girls have had four or more sexual partners. As a result, a million teenagers become pregnant each year while about three million adolescents contract sexually-transmitted diseases.

One possible solution is already beginning to be provided by young people themselves who have given up the permissive way of life in favor of a more puritanical outlook. At a recent mass rally in Washington D.C., thousands of teenagers assembled to declare that they would abstain from sex before marriage. Oprah Winfrey devoted one of her television shows to this topic in which several teenage girls spoke of regretting early sexual experience. Others saw maintaining their virginity as a way of remaining in control of their lives.

Strong feelings were evoked when one girl equated sexual abstinence with purity. Others were quick to point out that having sex does not render you unwholesome! Here was an outstanding example of the patriarchal prejudice against women's sexuality which is by no means confined to men. The general consensus among this group was that traditional sex education in its current form is unhelpful. They felt that more emphasis needs to be placed on the emotional rather than the purely physical aspects of sexuality. I found it altogether encouraging that the girls, at least, emphasized their wish to establish a loving relationship before becoming sexually involved with a man.

Our current antidote to the abuse of sexual power is political correctness. This I see as a form of twentieth-century Puritanism, the pendulum having swung right away from the permissiveness of the sixties. The concept itself, born of sad necessity, only serves to demonstrate how far we are from a state of mutual respect between the sexes. Some American universities have gone so far as to draw up codes of sexual practice, whereby a man must ask a woman's permission to touch her before each new stage of lovemaking. Nothing, it seems to me, could be more soulless or lacking in that essential ingredient, humor. And how can

François Mitterand's natural daughter, Mazarine, pictured at his funeral with her mother, the President's mistress Anne Pingeot (in mourning veil).

respect for others or self-respect be developed by obedience to a set of rules imposed by an outer authority? From a psychological point of view, not only does the very idea make no sense but we are in principle fairly and squarely back in Jehovah territory!

Yet "date rape" appears to be an increasing problem that must be addressed. I see no way forward except to look at the underlying cause of the problem. Rape is anathema to anybody who can relate well to others. If a man is both confident in his masculinity and on good terms with his feminine-feeling nature, he has no need to be sexually abusive, let alone to commit rape. Yet again, it comes back to issues of education and initiation. Women also have their lessons to learn if sexuality is to become less of a battleground and more of a mutual delight and sharing. For centuries, women, having no power of their own, learned to use their sexuality to manipulate the men who controlled them. For as long as they continue to do so, they will perpetuate the masculine fear of woman's power, which so often turns into the wish to control and punish the woman.

Everyone, whether male or female, needs to feel connected to life in a way which gives them dignity and self-respect. By retrieving the soul of sexuality, we would go a long way towards this end. We have seen how in some cultures, notably the Hindu, the two have always been linked. And the Taoist view, although not quite the same, at least makes sex an art form and explores its possibilities as a means of enlightenment. A movement in this direction is already afoot. Many ancient erotic mysteries are resurfacing, creating a new wave of sexuality. New books on Taoist and Tantric techniques by such writers and teachers as Jolen Chang are appearing in large numbers. Workshops and sexuality seminars are attracting growing interest in the USA and Europe. Participants learn to experience sacred sexuality by letting go of the need to perform or control so that lovemaking becomes a process of feeling and blending with the other. Where East meets West in this way, wholeness is possible.

At the other end of the scale is the ever-increasing growth of pornography. Where we are out of touch with our own personal myth, that sense of being connected to an underlying process that gives our lives meaning, we experience a vacuum that has to be filled. Pornography does this in a negative way. It is in fact the shadow side of the Puritan outlook. Where there is repression, guilt and fear on the surface, there will be powerfully lustful and sadistic impulses underneath. Pornography, which is

Sharon Stone with Michael Douglas in *Basic Instinct*, in which she personified the archetypal devouring feminine who first copulates with her victim and then kills him.

not at all the same thing as joyful, uninhibited sexuality, undoubtedly devalues and exploits women, a view with which I know many would disagree. It is true that where pornography meets mainstream cinema, a woman might be depicted as powerful. We have only to think of the part played by Sharon Stone in the film *Basic Instinct*. The character she plays specializes in killing the men she copulates with while they relax after orgasm. Although the story stands firmly within the tradition of the devouring feminine, I am not sure that the cause of harmony between the sexes is much helped by depicting a woman as a human praying mantis.

If we consider sexual activity in terms of the Indian system of energy centers called *chakras*, pornography focuses entirely on the lowest of these, situated at the base of the spine, creating an imbalance of energy which is in fact detrimental to emotional and spiritual health. Warm and related sexual experience is much deeper and causes energy to flow around the whole body. As sexual beings, we are more than our genitals. In due course, as we move into the twenty-first century and learn more about the subtle energies of the body, these things will become much more an accepted part of Western thinking.

On a more positive note, it seems to me that many people are unconsciously trying to access through pornography the kind of experience which was available in the ancient temples of the goddess. Aphrodite Porné had her place, and a valuable place it was. But sexual experience of this kind require an attitude of reverence for the energies involved, tenderness and appreciation as well as passion. A man did not visit the temple in order to abuse the priestess. On the contrary, he went in hope of an experience which would connect him to a powerful source of life-giving energy, an experience which pornography cannot provide.

We could go some way towards counteracting the need for pornography by adopting a different view of prostitution. Given that this is a phenomenon which has existed since ancient times and will inevitably continue to do so, how could it play a more creative part in our culture?

Here we could learn from the customs of the ancients. If the women offering their sexual services knew that what they were giving was, potentially, something of immense value and generally recognized as such, they and their customers alike would benefit in terms of enhanced consciousness and self-respect.

We are perhaps seeing the beginnings of such an attitude in the activities of a woman such as Annie Sprinkle in the USA. Ms. Sprinkle, who advertises herself as the "Multimedia Whore," appears in live and immensely popular performances where she masturbates to orgasm on stage, using a giant dildo. One of her acts involves inviting members of the audience to inspect her cervix through a speculum, an act which serves to place the

A marble relief dating from the 2nd century AD depicting Gaia, the personification of the Earth Mother.

performance on a different level than merely pornography. Ms. Sprinkle, who makes no secret of her earlier careers as prostitute and porn star, claims that her attitudes to sexuality were changed when she studied Tantra. She brings both honesty and humor to her work, her philosophy being that the greatest contribution she can make to life is to have as much fun and joy as possible. Ms. Sprinkle also runs workshops for women, where she encourages them to explore their sexual personalities by dressing up in provocative outfits. In mythological terms, she is a carrier of Aphrodite, helping both men and women to enjoy their sexual nature without guilt or false modesty.

The myth of the goddess is currently enjoying a revival in many ways. What began as a minority "New Age" interest in feminine spirituality, goddess worship and witchcraft, is becoming more generally widespread. But it is in the area of ecology where our need to honor feminine values is gaining increasing momentum. The earth is once more being understood as a living thing, Gaia, our Mother Earth, who, since the Industrial Revolution, has been consistently raped and maimed. Yet the very survival of mankind depends on her health and well-being. The Great Mother stands in need of urgent attention. For too long we have gone along with the puritanical masculine approach of transcending the body and somehow rising above the flesh. From such a standpoint, desecration of the earth is unimportant. Greenpeace, Friends of the Earth and other organizations are working hard to raise collective awareness in this area, trying to slow down the rate at which we deplete our natural resources so as to give them an opportunity to recover.

In the same way, we need to become aware of the need to heal the wounds of the feminine aspect of the psyche, the goddess within. Inner ecology requires that we honor our feelings and intuition and refuse to decimate them with our logic as chainsaws destroy the rain forests. Reason and logic have their place, of course. You cannot operate a computer without them. But they do not belong in the world of Eros, the realm of relatedness and the interplay of sexual energies. The new myths need to counteract the masculine view of the feminine as destructive and essentially negative, an attitude deep-rooted in the unconscious of the majority of men. An enlightened approach to sexuality, whereby men and women meet as equals who respect and value each other, could transform our lives and make life on Earth more closely resemble Heaven than Hell.

Prostitute turned performance artist, Annie Sprinkle, appearing as a Tantric divinity in *Rapture Season*, at the Institute of Contemporary Arts, London.

AUTHOR'S ACKNOWLEDGMENTS

I would like to thank the following people who have been particularly helpful to me when writing this book: Mary Anne Fitzgerald for her valuable contribution gained from her experience of living among the Samburu. Richard Craze for a wealth of information, especially in respect of Taoist and Tantric practices. Roni Jay and Kate Jay for allowing me access to unpublished thesis material about the Greek view of virginity. Richard Dening for many helpful suggestions and general encouragement.

Sarah Dening. BATTERSEA, LONDON 1996

The publishers would like to thank the following picture agencies for their permission to reproduce the illustrations in this book:

Ancient Art and Architecture Collection: Pages 1, 3, 6, 7, 10, 40, 41, 42, 46, 51, 55, 57, 62, 63, 64, 65, 71, 73, 78, 83, 85, 87, 90, 99, 105, 106, 134, 137, 143, 145, 147, 153, 154, 162, 163, 205, 217
Barnaby's Picture Library: 175
Bridgeman Picture Library: Pages 2, 43, 59, 66, 69, 79, 84, 86, 91, 94, 98, 102, 119, 126, 131, 133, 139, 159, 173, 182, front cover panel.
C. Lesley Spatt: 186
C. M. Dixon: 14, 49, 52
Guildhall Library/photo Jeremy Butler: 185
Hulton Deutsch Picture Library: 188, 209
Images Picture Library: 11, 12, 110, 113, 130, 135, 157, 167, 207
Kobal Picture Library: 200, 201, 215
The Mansell Collection: 68, 77, 81, 82, 141, 148, 152, 161, 165, 177, 179
Mary Evans Picture Library: 8, 9, 32, 117, 121, 125, 176, 190, 195
The National Gallery of Scotland: 43
Panos Pictures: 20, 21, 22, 24
Rapture Season: 219
Rex Features: 197, 199, 210, 213
Scala Picture Library: 150, 151
Sue Cunningham Photographic: 37, 18, 198
Trip: 26, 27, 31, 39, 60, 67, 75, 107, 111, 116, 123
Wellcome Institute: 61, 88, 93, 170, 181
Werner Forman Archive: PAGES 5, 23, 35, 95, 103
West Country Photos: 202

Index